GET
POSITIVE
LIVE
POSITIVE

DEDICATION

Archangel Michael, as you assisted me onto my path during one of my darkest days. *My sister, Melanie Ann,* who guides me gently from the Other Side. Thank you for helping me to recognize the opportunities. *My parents, Mary and Michael, my sister Michelle, my nephew Declan, and my grandmother Josephine*—thank you for all of your love and encouragement and for sharing in my excitement on this journey. Lastly, to *Riley*, the best and most spoiled rescue dog that brought the magic back into my life before crossing the Rainbow Bridge.

Melinda D. Carver

GET POSITIVE LIVE POSITIVE

*Clearing the Negativity
from Your Life*

REDFeather
MIND | BODY | SPIRIT
An Imprint of Schiffer Publishing, Ltd.

Published by Red Feather Mind Body Spirit
An Imprint of Schiffer Publishing, Ltd.
4880 Lower Valley Road
Atglen, PA 19310
Phone: (610) 593-1777; Fax: (610) 593-2002
E-mail: Info@schifferbooks.com
Web: www.schifferbooks.com

For our complete selection of fine books on this and related subjects, please visit our website at www.schifferbooks.com. You may also write for a free catalog.

Schiffer Publishing's titles are available at special discounts for bulk purchases for sales promotions or premiums. Special editions, including personalized covers, corporate imprints, and excerpts, can be created in large quantities for special needs. For more information, contact the publisher.

We are always looking for people to write books on new and related subjects. If you have an idea for a book, please contact us at proposals@schifferbooks.com.

CONTENTS

PART III:

Welcoming Positive Energy . . . 91

ACKNOWLEDGMENTS

I would like to acknowledge the following people who have brightened my path with their affection and support. Thank you for cheering as I walked boldly forward.

Marie McGovern, for your friendship and all of your non-stop support, guidance, and encouragement while I found the right path. My friends Sue Hastings, Nancy Ritz, Mary Nale, Yaffa Copeland, Joel Wertz, Candie Michelle Toska, and Sally Brustowicz for sharing the laughter, tears, and joy through the years.

Kelly Bowman, who loved my workshop and gave me the first opportunity to present it live at the Gift of Light Expo seven years ago! John Addison, of AVS Productions, who has included eleven of my workshops in his *Holistic Highway to Wisdom DVD Series*. My dearly departed friend, Ken Harsh, who was adamant in his belief that my workshop should be turned into a book.

Paulina Cassidy, for your hauntingly beautiful music that brightened my energy while I transformed my workshop into a book format. Stevie Nicks, for your songs that I rocked out to whenever I felt blocked throughout the various times in my life.

James Wanless, for including me in wonderful opportunities and for writing the foreword for my first book. Chris McClure, of Schiffer Publishing, for finding me at INATS and believing in me. Jerry Masek, for the professional photography session in the magical Cleveland Metroparks. My friend, Jill Mattson, for allowing me to use your beautiful artwork on my cover.

Thank you to dear Claudius—my Spirit Guide and Past Life mate—for supporting, guiding, and encouraging me once more during this lifetime. Yes, you have been right every time, as you laughingly state to me.

FOREWORD

by James M. Wanless, PhD

The number one issue in life is how we think about ourselves. Most of us have an inner critic who says we are not good enough, not smart enough, not good looking enough, just not enough. These negative thoughts about ourselves are the greatest demons of life. They destroy who we really are and who we are meant to be. They are deep, they are incessant, and they create—as you think, so you live.

I remember on my trek to the Himalayan Mountains in 1974, I fortunately spent a month in a Tibetan Buddhist monastery. Not only was I cured of hepatitis by the golden light meditations, I began the long journey of clearing the "negative mind." Every day we meditated on our negative self-talk. It was an enlightening wake-up call. Ever since, I have become like a cat on a mouse, constantly observing and catching my self-doubt and my self-criticism. To this day, I still pounce on the deadly demons of the negative mind.

The best thing you can do to enhance and improve your life is read this book and actively follow its advice! Melinda Carver gives you no nonsense, down-to-earth ways for clearing out the mental devils, which I believe exist within us so that we can truly appreciate who we are and who we can be. This greatest lesson and challenge of all is your golden opportunity to transform your life, evolve, and be all that you can be.

What has really helped me vanquish the negativities is to understand that we are creatures of habit like all organisms. So, to rid yourself of a habitual and dysfunctional way of negative self-talk requires establishing a new habit, a positive way of conversing and thinking about yourself. The next time you catch your inner critic, use that as a catalyst that triggers new self-talk that is healthy and positive. Don't just get rid of the thought-demons, engage the thought-angels, perhaps like Melinda's Archangel Michael, with a positive affirmation. Hear yourself say to yourself, that you are enough, plenty enough, and that you *can* and that you *are* a person of the light who has the power to walk in beauty and make your world a loving place. To make this "switch of habits," it's imperative to have a picture of what changing your language about yourself will do for you. Keep visualizing your success that happens by changing your old thought patterns. This visualization is a surefire motivator that will sustain your cleansing efforts.

Remember, this is a lifelong endeavor, not a quick overnight, take a pill and everything is okay. This is your everyday spiritual path and practice. Of all yogis and spiritual disciplines, this is by far the most essential for a happy, healthy, wealthy, and holy life. Thank you to Melinda for giving you the nitty-gritty mechanics of living the whole and sustainable life!

—James M. Wanless, PhD
Author of *Voyager Tarot*, *Way of the Great Oracle*,
Sustain Yourself Cards, and *Intuition @ Work*.

PREFACE

The Birth of Get Positive Live Positive:
Clearing the Negativity from Your Life

When the recession struck the USA, I was laid off from my administrative assistant job. I would scour job postings daily, send resumes, go on interviews, and network. Hearing the dreaded "too qualified" or "this is for a beginner, you'll be bored" over and over after interviews was just so soul-crushing. One month turned into three months, and I was still jobless. I had never been out of work for so long. It was demoralizing, disheartening, and scary.

At the fourth month mark of being jobless, I awoke and turned on my computer to begin the daily chore of searching all of the job websites. In my inbox, several e-mails awaited me. Wow, I thought, I received many responses today. Nine new e-mails from companies! I couldn't wait to read them. The first one was a rejection, followed by eight more rejection letters. Nine rejections—all in one day—was a new record for me. Turning off the computer, I went running back to bed to cry under the covers. It felt like I was stuck in the muck.

Both my dad, who was staying with me at the time, and my dog Riley were knocking on my door. My dad asked me what was wrong. I told him about the nine rejections and that I was too depressed to talk and just wanted to be left alone. Riley was by the bed trying to give me kisses. I was inconsolable and asked them to just let me be.

As I lay there, I wondered what would happen. What if I could not find a new job? What if I lost my house? No apartment would take my 135-pound dog, Riley. He loved his yard. How would I buy food? I just cried harder. All of a sudden, I felt this poke in my side and a voice said, "Get up; go back to your computer." Being under the covers still, I thought it was my dad. "Dad, just leave me alone." The voice boomed out, "Get up. There's much to do." I whipped the covers up ready to yell at dad. I looked around, no dad in the room. I yelled, "Whoever you are, leave me alone," and I crawled back under the covers.

Twice more I was poked on my side and told to get up. I ignored the voice. Finally, an exasperated voice said, "I am Archangel Michael; you know many ways to help people, and you must get up and write. Your misery is setting you on your path; it's time to begin." I laughed and figured I was going crazy from the crying jag. "What path?" I asked. "Prove to me that you are Archangel Michael."

A warm blue light filled my room just above my bed—I could see it through my covers. A sword held in a hand appeared, followed by a masculine shape. Dozens of thoughts flickered through my brain—the many times I saw him when I was young, the dangerous night he gave me courage when I was out of town in my early twenties. I had not seen Archangel Michael since that night. More symbols, objects, and words flew around. I squeezed my eyes shut and said, "No, I don't want to go back to the computer. I just want to lay here." Archangel Michael prodded me with his sword once again, telling me, "It's time, Melinda; get up."

I flipped up the covers, asking him if I typed what he was prodding me to do, would he leave me alone so I could go back to bed? He laughed, loud and long. Archangel Michael said, "No, I will not be far from you today. Now get up; you already know what you will write." Huffily, I got up and went back to my office. I started writing about lemons, crystals, colors, herbs, and much more. For thirty minutes, I just typed away while Michael looked around. He made comments about my decorating, my snarled hair, and how it was good and right for me to begin on my correct life path to start helping people.

My first workshop, "Clearing the Negativity from Your Life!" was born that morning. Then I began researching expos or fairs to present it. I began sending e-mails out to show promoters and metaphysical groups to introduce myself with a mini-summary of my workshop. I couldn't believe what I was doing. That afternoon, I received a phone call from a promoter, Kelly Bowman, in Columbus. We spoke for a long time. She put me on her expo's lecture list that was happening in two weeks. Michael told me it was all in order, that this is what I needed to do.

During dinner, Dad asked me what I was working on. When I told him I wrote a workshop and was e-mailing people to present it to, he was shocked and worried. He felt I should concentrate on finding a job. After dinner, I started pulling ingredients and mixing them. I created my Fairy Dust (brings Joy and Happiness) and Cosmic Dust (clears Negative Energy) that night. By the time I went to bed, I had created a workshop, was booked to speak at a metaphysical expo in two weeks, and created two of my products. I was energized, on a roll, and still had Archangel Michael hanging around. Not once did I think about those nine rejection letters.

In that one day, I had experienced the deepest, darkest despair and then turned that into the start of a new, exciting future. Slowly, with Archangel Michael's prodding, I had pulled myself out of the muck. It was my time of rebirth.

By starting on my path as a professional psychic medium, teaching workshops, and creating products, I have found a new happiness in my life. This is what I was meant to do now. This is what I have done in most of my past lives. You too can pull yourself out of the muck of deepest despair. Which Archangel will come to prod you? Mine was Archangel Michael. I am forever grateful that he showed up that day.

INTRODUCTION

Congratulations! You have just made a productive, positive step in changing your life by purchasing this book. My book will teach you how negativity enters into your life and affects every aspect: your attitude, emotions, relationships, and career. This negativity also sabotages your manifesting abilities and reduces your energy vibrations.

Once you know HOW you attract and create it, you will discover the free or inexpensive tools and steps to assist you in clearing negativity from every aspect of your life. The free tools listed within will allow you to begin today as you are reading this book. The other tools listed might be in your house or garden already. Others may require a quick trip to a metaphysical, religious, or grocery store. By using both the free and inexpensive tools, you will double your ability to clear negativity from your life.

You will also explore ways to create and allow positive energy to flow around you by breaking negative patterns and raising your energy vibrations. Imagine how happier and healthier you can be without negativity dragging you down. Imagine the positive life that you can build starting right now. Knowledge is power. The more you know, the more effective you will become in living in positive energy. Empowering you to assist yourself to do so is the underlying principle of my book.

I have studied metaphysics for over twenty years, including the spirit world, energy vibrations, and magic. As a professional psychic medium, I have provided counseling sessions for thousands of people worldwide. Not only have I connected them with their deceased loved ones, guides, and angels, I have also assisted them with their life issues. Beside the ability to communicate with the spirit world, I can see and work within my clients' energy streams. Through these sessions, I have developed as a Positive Energy Specialist. These are the lessons that I have learned throughout my life and derived from my clients' lives. These are the tools that I have used to combat negativity in my own life and have recommended to my clients for their use.

I have written this book to teach you how to clear the negative energy from your life in all forms. You do not have to suffer through negativity. You do not have to accept negative energy from yourself or from others. I want to teach you how to create positive energy and empower your intentions so that you may welcome positive people, opportunities and events into your life. I want you to live in positive energy with the highest vibrations and intentions so you may create the most beautiful life for yourself. You are a spiritual being having a human existence. You deserve to evolve with the highest, purest, positive vibrations supporting you. Get positive, live positive!

Part I

NEGATIVITY ENTERS

The Five Variants

CHAPTER 1

THE FIRST VARIANT = YOU

Have you been feeling more tired and irritable lately? Do you have poor results while trying to manifest your dreams into reality? Have you felt the need to get out of your house more? Do you hide from your family? Are you fighting with your spouse or lover all the time? Are the issues with your neighbors escalating? Is your work place really bearing down on you? Do you have to talk yourself into walking into that building every day?

If you have felt these emotions or are experiencing these problems, you are feeling the effects of negative energy in your life. Many people go through their lives angry, depressed, anxious, or upset. They live in this negative energy all the time. They are on antidepressants, antianxiety pills, and take anger management courses. These negative emotions pull your energy into a very low vibration.

The more you are drained and stressed by this negative energy, the more negative energy flows into your life. You attract what you are; you attract energy at a level that you yourself are vibrating at. No one wants to feel depressed, stressed, or angry. We want to feel happy, positive, and

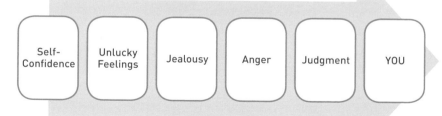

vibrant. We want to feel alive and joyful. We want control of our intentions and vibrations.

What causes this negativity to enter? There are five variants that cause negativity to enter into all facets of your life. You will recognize these variants if you have read advice columns in the newspaper regularly or overheard a very loud cell phone conversation at the grocery store or if you participated in group discussions with your family or friends.

The first variant is YOU. Yes, you! Most people do not realize that they cause and attract the most negativity by going about their day. Your energy is like a magnet; you draw or repel others with your energy. How is your energy like a magnet? The way that you feel about yourself radiates from you. Your behavior—the way you act toward others or in front of others also radiates from you. Your energy will then attract that same vibration to you, or repel it away from you. Your energy vibration also affects the power of your intentions to manifest the life that you want.

As a human, you have Free Will for your behavior and feelings. Your thoughts are made of energy; speaking those thoughts will amplify that energy. You are the only one responsible for your thoughts, words, actions, and reactions. You have the power to either be in a negative vibration—which brings you negative emotions, people, and events. You also have the power to be in a positive vibration—which will bring you positive emotions, people, and events.

Let us look at some of the ways that you create negativity for yourself in your everyday life. Many of you will see yourselves in these variants and have that "ah-ha!" moment.

Having Low Self-Confidence or Self Esteem

When you have low self-confidence or low self-esteem, you radiate a low-level vibration. This vibration hums very softly and can be ignored by others. You do not feel good about yourself. You do have a very low amount of self-love. This is the most basic beginning of allowing negative energy into your life.

It is evident to others when you have low self-confidence or self-esteem. You try not to attract attention from family, friends, or coworkers. You hide your intelligence or sense of humor. You may choose to not participate in social functions or work events. You may also make self-depreciating comments about yourself to others or not accept compliments.

Other people will respond to you based on the energy that you emit. If you are putting out "stay away" or "don't look at me" vibrations, then that is exactly what others will do! Your energy attracts the energy of people, opportunities, and events.

EXAMPLE

You walk into a party. You immediately notice one woman standing in a group of four others. This woman is laughing, chatting with others easily, and holding her glass of wine away from her body. This woman is confident. She is friendly and is emitting a high vibration. You look around the rest of the room and notice another woman sitting quietly on the couch by herself. Her shoulders are hunched forward and she holds her glass of wine against her chest. This woman's eyes dart around the room but never make contact with anyone else. She is quiet and emitting a low vibration. Now, which woman would you like to be introduced to?

Most of you will be drawn to the confident, high-vibrating woman. Her energy is welcoming and positive. A few of you might feel bad for the woman on the couch, and you will try to have a conversation with her. However, her energy is repelling you so that you only stay with her for a few minutes before rising off the couch to speak to others. This example shows vividly why your self-confidence is important. Other people will treat you the same way that you treat yourself!

Feeling Unlucky or Less Fortunate

Some of you just feel "unlucky" or less fortunate than other people in your life. You wonder why you have not won the lottery or that big horse race. You watch movies and TV and wonder why you do not have designer bags, expensive cars, or a castle with a moat. This feeling of having less all of the time will allow in negative energy. It makes you feel less than others in your life.

You walk around believing that you are unlucky and then announce to others that you are unlucky. Guess what? You will remain unlucky! Your thoughts are energy and by speaking those thoughts out loud, you amplify that energy. You are telling God or the Universe that YOU are unlucky, keep me this way. By stating this over and over, you are keeping that low vibration around you. That negative vibration reverberates from every pore of your being.

EXAMPLE

You play bingo with Betty every Wednesday at the church. You pick up Betty and state, "I never win at bingo; you always do!" You have just told God or the Universe (depending on your belief system) that you NEVER win, so now you will not win. Betty laughs lightly replying, "Yes, I am lucky! I wear my lucky bracelet every week." Betty is telling God or the Universe that she is lucky and welcomes abundance.

Betty allows her vibration to flow in "luck" or abundance. Whether she wins a free bingo card, a dauber, or the big bingo pot, Betty flows in positive energy. This positive energy works like a magnet for Betty. You, on the other hand, state negative thoughts and, therefore, flow in negative energy. For more information on this topic, please see the Natural Laws chapter in this book.

Extreme Jealousy of Others

We are all spiritual beings having a human experience. In our human bodies, we have human emotions of anger, pettiness, vindictiveness, and jealousy. Some small amount of jealousy is normal, we are human after all. However, when you allow jealousy to consume you, it opens the door to negative energy.

Jealousy is the feeling of having less than someone else—of being inferior. You are not happy with your life, your relationship, or your career when you compare it to someone else's. Jealousy is also competitive and the person you are jealous of does not even realize you WANT to compete against them.

> You are married to a sweet man, live in a modest house, and have two children that are average students. However, you are extremely jealous of your sister-in-law. Her house is larger, her husband makes more money, she dresses in designer clothing, and her three children make the honor roll. You compare your husband's looks and actions to her husband—then feel your husband is less than her husband. You compare the Chevrolet that you drive to her Mercedes and feel aggravated that her car costs more.

The extreme jealousy that you feel for your sister-in-law festers and grows in strength every year. This jealousy, this competition that you have set inside your head, is not healthy. It allows negative energy to flow into your life. This energy affects your life in all ways because you are not happy or grateful for what you have. You want something that someone else has.

Extreme Anger

Anger is a natural emotion. It comes from deep within when you feel you are treated unfairly, disrespectfully, or when someone did something very wrong to you. What is not normal is extreme anger—people who are angry about every little thing in their lives. Every day you see these people who walk through life with a huge chip on their shoulder.

These people will overreact to small issues or problems that crop up. Nothing makes them happy or calms them down. This extreme anger will bring in negative energy.

> Joe walks through life with a bad attitude and a chip on his shoulder. He works at the local factory and applies for the foreman position. Joe's bosses review his employment file. It is filled with small, petty arguments with his coworkers and perceived slights from management. The big boss promotes another employee who has an exemplary record and the ability to lead a team.

Joe is enraged because he felt he deserved this promotion. He has worked at the company longer and has been cross-trained. Joe feels that he has been slapped in the face by being passed over for the promotion. Joe storms into the big boss' office and screams and threatens him. Joe is then fired for making threats.

The Judging Busybody

Judging others for their appearance, personality quirks, temperament, homes, cars, and other possessions is a worldwide phenomenon. No matter where you go to in any country, people will look at you and make quick judgments about you. They usually keep their judgments to themselves or mention it to their partner. Many people feel this is a matter-of-course event and do not bat an eye. However, some people will take this to the extreme!

There are people in this world who will look at your appearance or your habits or your mistakes and shout their judgment of you from the rooftops. This extreme form of judging turns the person judging you into a busybody. They make their judgment and then broadcast to everyone they know to attempt to gain a "consensus" against you. They want to blacken your reputation and to make themselves look good by comparison, even if the person judging has done what you are doing! Many people favor the concept of "do as I say, not as I do."

EXAMPLE

Kate is the mother of Abby, a fourteen-year-old girl. She is one of those extreme "helicopter" parents watching everything that Abby does. You are hosting a birthday party for your fourteen-year-old son. He invites Abby and ten other friends. You and your husband are in and out of the room, keeping an eye on what is happening with the kids.

When Abby arrives home, Kate gives her the third degree on who was there, what was served, what activities happened, and whether alcohol and drugs were involved. Abby describes the food and guests and that no drugs or alcohol were at the party. Kate keeps digging and Abby tells her that a boy and a girl both kissed in front of everyone during a game. Abby also tells Kate that watching the kiss made her uncomfortable.

Kate starts calling the parents of the other guests to tell them that you and your husband were not always watching the children and that kissing games were going on. She insinuates that other activities may have happened. She is on the warpath and wants to blacken you and your husband's reputation with the other parents. The other parents laughingly call you to tell you what Kate is saying about two fourteen year olds kissing. You assure the other parents that you were never gone from the room for longer than five minutes. The other parents tell you that this is not the first time Kate has made her calls about someone else's behavior. They do not think very highly of her and you no longer allow Abby to come to your home for your son's events.

Kate is stuck in negative energy and is throwing it all around you and your husband. This will steamroll into bigger issues for Kate and Abby as you and other parents and their kids shun Abby to avoid Kate.

You change your physical and aura energy by your thoughts about yourself, your attitude, and your mood. Your behaviors also influence the energy that you live in. Once again, you are responsible for your own thoughts, words, actions, and reactions. You are the main variant for allowing negative energy to affect every facet of your life.

If you do not feel good about yourself, others will not either. It is your attitude pattern that must be changed. When you are extremely jealous of others or angry at people, you will send out negativity. If you are practicing intense judgments of people, you will flow in negativity. If you concentrate on only what you lack in your life, you will attract negative patterns.

Pulling yourself out of these patterns will allow positive energy and feelings to grow within you and emanate from you. Building your self-confidence and loving yourself will raise your vibrations. These two actions will help you to break the patterns listed above.

Confidence exudes a positive vibration. It attracts people to you. Loving yourself elevates your vibration. When you love yourself, you then exude love and can then attract more love into your life.

What's Your Energy?

To assist you in determining whether or not your own energy is contributing negatively to your life, ask yourself the following questions. Space has been provided for you to write your answers.

1. How do you feel about yourself right now?

_____

_____

_____

2. Do you believe your feelings about yourself are positive or negative?

_____

_____

_____

3. In which way does your self esteem affect your manifesting?

_____

_____

_____

4. Do you say out loud or to others that you are "unlucky"? How often?

_____

_____

_____

5. Are you extremely jealous of another person right now?

_____

_____

_____

6. Have your emotions lately been stuck in "anger" mode? Are others afraid of you?

_____

_____

_____

7. Have you been attempting to bully another person?

_____

_____

_____

8. Describe to yourself how the actions above are impacting your life right now in a positive or negative manner.

_____

_____

_____

CHAPTER 2

THE SECOND VARIANT = YOUR PARTNER

Your partner—whether he or she is your spouse, lover, boyfriend, or girlfriend—can bring negative energy into your life in several ways. The reason your partner affects your energy is because any person that you have sex with does affect your energy. By allowing someone into your personal energy field (or aura), and by exchanging energy via sex, they leave an energy cord within your energy field. Because the act of sex is so intimate in so many ways, the energy of both of you connects and entwines. This is why choosing a partner is so important.

Energy exchanges and combinations of those closest to you do affect you. Your partner is the one person who has the most effect on you. People allow their emotions to ebb and flow based on this energy. Love, affection, trust, and loyalty are tightly entwined. Negativity is the number one killer of love relationships.

Let us review some of the ways your partner brings negative energy into your life.

THE SECOND VARIANT = YOUR PARTNER

Control — Arguments — Possession — PARTNER

Controlling Your Actions

If you have low self-esteem, you may choose a partner with a more forceful personality. A partner like this may attempt to control you and your actions. He or she overpowers your sense of self, slowly at first, but then their control becomes complete. You may feel that you cannot do anything or go anywhere without their approval.

He or she may attempt to isolate you from your family and friends. He or she may want to know your every move throughout your day. They may ask questions similar to:

- What time do you leave work?
- Why does your car mileage show that you stopped somewhere?
- Where did you stop? Did you meet someone?

By having to account for every minute of your day, their control is complete.

This need to control you may also veer into verbal abuse. He or she may tell you that every word out of your mouth is wrong. Your partner may tell you that you cannot cook meals or clean the house to their satisfaction. They may also tell you that you are stupid, lazy, or no good without them to guide you or prod you. By criticizing and belittling you, they in turn ramp up their control of you. This brings negative energy into your life.

William and Tameka have just started dating. Tameka is flattered when William places his arm around her shoulder at all the events they attend. He begins to make comments about her friends or her other activities that keep her "away from him." He states that he wants to spend more time with her. He requests that she skip her monthly dine-around club and to stop her weekly girl's night out. Tameka skips the first dinner and night out.

William's requests to spend more time with him and less with her friends turn into demands. He begins isolating her from family, friends, and business associates. Tameka now cannot speak to others or attend events without William being there with her. Tameka's self-esteem begins to plummet when William's negative comments about her appearance and intelligence become a thrice-a-day event. This relationship is saturated with negative energy and will continue to worsen.

Sometimes this verbal abuse becomes physical abuse. If you are ever hit, punched, kicked, or beaten, you should take steps to safely leave your partner. Physical abuse never stops, it only escalates.

If you are experiencing physical abuse, contact your local police department or call the National Domestic Violence Hotline at 1-800-799-7233 to develop a safe escape plan.

Constant Arguments—Not Getting Along

Another way that negative energy enters into your love relationships is by constant arguments. We do not always agree with our partner, nor can we compromise all of the time. That is normal. What is not normal is having the same argument over and over until you are sick of it, or not being able to compromise on ANY issue.

When you argue all of the time, the love and affection that you have for your partner may whither each time. The more you fill your love relationship with negative energy, the less love and positive energy can remain. You will begin to dislike your partner. This dislike grows until there is a severe loss in the relationship—whether it is loss of love, affection, sex, or the relationship itself. Negativity is the number one killer of love relationships.

> Bill and Susan have young pre-school age children. Bill wants to send the children to a private religious school. He believes their education will be enhanced at a more structured school. Susan wants to send the children to the local public school. She believes they will make friends with a larger group of students. Bill and Susan argue about where to send the children every week. Each time that they argue, Bill's voice becomes louder and Susan brings up other issues in their relationship.

This constant series of week-in and week-out arguments affects their relationship. Negative energy creeps in, with both feeling less affection and a lower sexual drive. They both begin arguing about additional issues in their lives. Bill and Susan stop kissing hello and goodbye and have less sex.

> Leroy has been dating Denise for the past six months. They both have met each other's friends. However, Leroy does not like Denise's friend, Nicole. He feels that Nicole is disrespectful of him and his relationship with Denise. Denise always invites Nicole to dinner each week, and they also double date with Nicole and her boyfriend. Nicole makes rude comments, and Leroy has to bite his tongue. Leroy has told Denise several times that he does not enjoy spending time with Nicole and that she is rude and mean. Denise defends Nicole and tells Leroy he just has to accept Nicole.

Without a resolution, these arguments fill the relationship with negative energy. Denise begins to nitpick at Leroy for other small comments and behaviors. Leroy's aggravation continues to grow. Finally, Leroy ends the relationship with Denise.

Possessiveness

Sometimes you choose a partner who has very low self-esteem or who has been emotionally stunted from past relationships. This partner will exhibit the "clinginess" gene of possessiveness. They want to know what you are thinking about when you look at someone passing by on the street. They become jealous that you hugged your sister goodbye. They become upset that you have to work late with an attractive coworker.

Partners who show possessiveness may appear flattering at first. However, this possessive partner eventually is not fun to be around. Their extreme, dramatic reaction to innocent conversations or signs of affection for others causes great negative energy to flow into your relationship.

> Nicole has been dating Kevin for six months. Kevin is close to his two older sisters. He always greets his sisters with a peck on the cheek. During the holidays, Kevin brings Nicole to meet his family. She becomes highly upset that Kevin kissed his sisters hello and that they are gently ribbing each other. Nicole feels that he should not kiss any other woman except his mom.
>
> During the same visit home, Kevin and Nicole run into his high school girlfriend, Lisa, and her husband. Lisa introduces her husband and kids to Kevin and Nicole. Nicole flips out on Kevin after the family leaves because she feels that Kevin should have nothing to do with a past girlfriend. After they return from this holiday visit, Kevin breaks off his relationship with Nicole because he cannot handle her dramatic reactions any more.

When you have a toxic partner or argue often, it not only brings negative energy into your relationship, it will cause a loss of affection or attraction. Most people grow apart due to this loss of passion toward their partner. It is very hard to repair relationships that experience this negative energy. Both partners really have to work on fixing their energy and the energy of the relationship.

Some of these relationships are not able to be repaired. When a partner is creating non-stop negative energy within the relationship, you must decide whether you want to stay in that toxic situation. Sometimes it is best to dissolve toxic love relationships. Releasing toxic partners from your life will allow you to heal. You cannot control your partner, nor can you make them "change." They are responsible for their own thoughts, words, actions, and reactions.

You deserve to have a loving, healthy, and supportive relationship. You deserve to have a positive, loving partner in your life.

What's Your Energy?

To assist you in determining whether or not your partner's energy is contributing negatively to your life, ask yourself the following questions. Space has been provided for you to write your answers.

1. How do you feel about your partner right now?

_____

_____

_____

2. Do you believe that your feelings for your partner are positive or negative?

_____

_____

_____

3. In which ways does your partner attempt to control your behavior?

_____

_____

_____

4. Which issue(s) do you and your partner consistently argue about?

_____

_____

_____

5. Why do you both continue to argue about this subject?

_____

_____

_____

6. Are you possessive of your partner? If so, how do you show possession?

_____

_____

_____

7. Is your partner possessive of you? If so, which ways do they show it?

_____

_____

_____

8. Describe how the actions listed above are impacting your life right now in a positive or negative manner.

_____

_____

_____

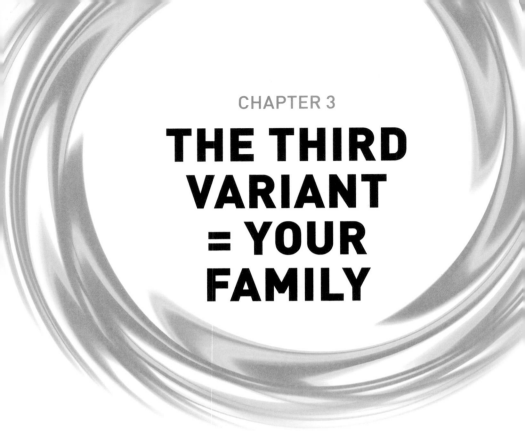

CHAPTER 3

THE THIRD VARIANT = YOUR FAMILY

You love your family—your mom, dad, siblings, grandparents, cousins, etc. Just as your partner can affect your energy field, so does your family. You believe that family is everything, and you strive to be the good son, daughter, brother, sister, cousin, etc. For most of us, family is great to have; a blessing to us. For others, family members can be toxic due to their comments, behaviors, and energy. Many people around the world spend countless hours in therapy due to family issues.

Many people are affected in horrible ways by the words or actions of family members. Sometimes these words or actions are innocently stated but still cause hurt feelings. Most family members may apologize for unkind comments or comments taken the wrong way.

At other times, the words and actions of a family member are intentional or used for manipulative purposes. The family member may be cruel, unkind, unloving, and toxic towards you in every way, every time they see you. These family members are the ones you dread seeing at holidays, picnics, and special events. They ruin your party, your wedding, or just the day itself.

THE THIRD VARIANT = YOUR FAMILY

| Arguments | Judgment | Know-It-All | FAMILY |

Let us review some of the ways your family creates negative energy in your life.

Arguments—Not Getting Along

As with your partner, negative energy enters into your family relationships via constant arguments. We will not always agree with our family, nor can we compromise on each issue. That is normal. What is not normal is having the same argument all of the time, or not being able to compromise on ANY issue.

The love and affection that you have for your family member will lessen over time due to constant arguments. The more you fill your family relationship with negative energy, the less love and the less positive energy can remain. You will begin to dislike your family member. This dislike continues to grow until you feel a loss of love and affection for that family member.

EXAMPLE

You and your brother are complete opposites. You enjoy sports and he enjoys traveling to exotic locations. You both have opposing political views. At each family event, whether it is a birthday, wedding, or funeral, you both raise your voices and shout at each other. You call each other horrible names and rehash things that upset you from childhood. This continues for thirty minutes each time the behavior starts. After thirty minutes, one of you storms out of the party.

A family event just cannot be pleasant for the rest of the family due to your constant arguments with your brother. This allows negative energy into your life. It affects your brotherly relationship and then begins altering your other family relationships.

The Bigot in the Family

We have no control of who is part of our family, and we cannot control family members' thoughts and opinions. The opinions that family members state about you, your relationships, your job, etc., can also affect you negatively. The most negative family member is the bigot—the one who makes his or her abusive or nasty opinions known about the way you are living your life. They will disparage you, your spouse, or partner, or your children due to race, sexual orientation, or religious differences.

Dealing with a bigot in the family—no matter his or her age—is quite difficult. Stopping his or her negativity is hard to do because other family members may quietly agree with him or her. Other family members may want to brush it aside so that they can continue having a good time regardless of your hurt feelings or tears. A bigot is a truly toxic person.

EXAMPLE

Your Uncle Jerry has always called people by vile nicknames. He has one for each culture, and he says the nicknames loudly and proudly at each event. Problems begin when you begin dating someone from another background. You bring your new partner with you to family functions. Uncle Jerry begins his normal rants, including jabs about the race of your partner. You and other family members tell him to stop, yet he continues. Your partner is near to tears due to this treatment and wants to leave.

You speak to your uncle by telephone after the event, and warn him to change his behavior. He says he is going to state his opinions and will not change. You then have to decide whether you will attend other upcoming events or whether you will continue to invite him to your own events. It is a vicious circle.

The Know-It-All

Every family has a know-it-all. This is often the person who will tell you that you are raising your children in the wrong manner or religion, or that your wedding needs to be planned a different way. Unlike the bigot, the know-it-all is trying to be "helpful" by giving their advice. However, they give advice all of the time, and it is quite unasked for! When you repeatedly hear that you are "doing it the wrong way," you will start second-guessing yourself. When you hear this all of the time, it will become negative energy due to the criticism heaped on you—thereby lowering your self esteem.

EXAMPLE

> Your sister-in-law, Jennie, has been married to your brother for years and their children are older teens. You have recently become a mother and are following your pediatrician's advice on a feeding schedule. Jennie states this is all wrong and that you must do it the way she previously has. She points out that she raised three kids and knows what she's talking about. She piles on the advice and becomes argumentative when you state your feelings.
>
> Jennie then becomes critical of the way you are feeding your baby, dressing your baby, and how you are holding your child. You begin to second guess yourself, and your husband does not get involved because she's "your brother's wife." Other family members begin to comment following Jennie's lead. You have just been slammed by a negative energy blast.

Dealing with toxic family members or issues can be daunting and very draining. Negative family situations affect not only you but other family members as they try to decide what to do about the issue. Some of them will choose to ignore the situation and carry on with the event. Others will choose sides, escalating the issue between you and the family member. Yet others will tell you to knock it off and say you are sorry so that "everyone can have a nice time."

It is up to you to calmly decide how you want to handle family issues with toxic relatives. You may choose to state your feelings and demand an apology. You may receive it, or you may not. You may choose to cut off all contact with the offending relative. This creates a new pattern for you. You are shielding yourself from further emotional harm. Be advised that other members of your family may attempt to bring harmony between you and your relative. Do not allow them to push you into "fixing" a relationship if you do not wish to be around toxic family members.

What's Your Energy?

To assist you in determining whether or not your family's energy is contributing negatively to your life, ask yourself the following questions. Space has been provided for you to write your answers.

1. How do you feel about your family right now?

_____

_____

_____

2. Do you believe that your feelings for your family members are positive or negative?

_____

_____

_____

3. In which ways does your family attempt to control your behavior?

_____

_____

_____

4. Which issue(s) does your family consistently argue about?

_____

_____

_____

5. Why do you and your family continue to argue about this subject?

_____

_____

_____

6. Do you feel bullied by your family's pronouncements or actions?

_____

_____

_____

7. Would you prefer less contact with a certain family member? Which one and why?

_____

_____

_____

8. Describe how the actions listed above are impacting your life right now in a positive or negative manner.

_____

_____

_____

CHAPTER 4

THE FOURTH VARIANT = YOUR HOME & YARD

Your home and your yard both allow negative energy into your life. Yes, these inanimate objects can also make you feel tired, stressed, and unhappy. How do inanimate objects, like your home or yard, create negative energy? It is simple really. You LIVE there. Also living with you in this home are your partner, kids, or other family members.

When you have disagreements, squabbles, and altercations with your partner or family, it creates negative energy. When you have these issues in your home or yard, the negative energy you create together stays in that home or yard. This negative energy lives in your home or yard with you and your family. It pulses and grows in strength as disagreements and fights happen. It will escalate with each new act of pettiness or aggression. This negativity will attract MORE negative energy.

As your home and yard fills itself with the negativity created by you and your family, it will attract more negativity. Cleaning your house by vacuuming or dusting will not remove it. Opening your windows to air

THE FOURTH VARIANT = YOUR HOME & YARD

| Home Energy | Yard Energy | Neighbors | HOME & YARD |

out your home will not remove it. Having someone sweep out your vents will not remove it. Negative energy is there and it will not leave until you clear it out.

The House's Energy

Your home is an inanimate object, but it does contain energy. The energy of the location contains the energy of what has happened in the past on the property and the energy of what YOU are creating in it. This energy in your home can make you more depressed, stressed, or unhappy. It will affect you in all ways and it will affect the relationships you have with those who live with you.

EXAMPLE

Growing up, you had two best friends. At the first friend's house, you were warmly welcomed, fed lunch and popsicles, and generally had a great time. The house felt good to you; you enjoyed being there and had a lot of fun. At the second friend's house, you always felt unwelcome by the family. You would only spend short amounts of time there, or you would become sick after being there. Your parents would have to pick you up from sleepovers in the middle of the night due to stomach issues or fears.

The first house you loved visiting, the second one not at all. As a child, you may not have known that you were reacting to the energy of the house. This is why you could not finish the sleepover, because being in that house made you physically ill.

> You are house hunting. You find two beautifully decorated houses online and set up a time to see them. As you walk into the first house, it feels "cold" to you. It does not feel welcoming, nor does it feel like a happy place to live. You ask the realtor why the house is being sold and she says "divorce." You stay only a short time and go to the next house.
>
> At the second house, you feel comfortable immediately. The house has a warm, loving energy, and you feel that this is a house that you can live in. Even though the second house may be five years older or a little short on the square footage, you prefer this house. The second house is the one you bid on.

This example illustrates how a house's energy will be felt by those who live or visit there. At the first house, the couple fought all of the time, filling it with negative energy. The energy repulsed you, making you feel cold. At the second house, the family expressed love and had many happy times there. The energy was positive and welcoming.

Which of these houses would be easier to sell in a soft housing market? It would definitely be the second house that would sell first.

The Yard's Energy

Energy from your physical house does spill into your yard. This negative energy will affect any parties, barbeques, or other events that you host in your yard. This negative energy will also affect your trees, bushes, gardens, and flowers. Fairies and elementals will avoid your yard due to negativity. They prefer warm, positive energy to work their magic. You probably do not like sitting outside or you may not be able to relax when you are in the yard.

You are hosting a Fourth of July picnic at your home. You have purchased the food, drinks, and decorations. The yard has been mowed and cleaned up. All is set for your family and friends. Everyone arrives, and the grill is fired up. The grill is not the only thing on fire today. Petty squabbles break out among the children over the toys, and the adults bicker over religion, politics, and beer brands.

Negative energy thrums through the air, causing friction and fights. You stare wide-eyed and wonder why your family and friends are arguing at your picnic when they never act this way at other picnics. You begin to get upset and start yelling at everyone to calm down and to stop arguing. Chaos begins and people start grabbing their children and food to leave. Thus begins the end of your picnic.

You spend time digging and tilling an area to make into a garden behind your garage. You spend a lot of money on buying seedlings and planting them. You water, fertilize, and weed your garden. However, the vegetables are slow to grow or, if they grow, they are not as full as your neighbor's garden. You check with your neighbor and find out that you bought your seedlings at the same location and are using the same fertilizer.

The difference in vegetable growth and lushness is due to the energy of your yard. Negativity will inhibit the plant growth, whereas the positive energy in your neighbor's yard encourages the vegetables to grow.

Neighbor Problems

Negativity affects people that live near you, not just those living with you. If you are experiencing major or minor problems with your neighbors, these incidents will affect the energy in your yard. Relations with your neighbors may worsen through negativity, nasty comments, or rude behaviors. The issues may either be caused by bad behavior from one or both of you, or by the energy emanating from the yard.

EXAMPLE

You fight with your spouse often and yell at your children. You also live next door to a retired couple who take great pride in their yard. Their lawn, bushes, and flowers are pristine. You send your children outside to play and do not watch them as closely now that they are a little older. They both have bikes and ride up and down your driveway and down the block. When they return, both your kids ride their bikes over the neighbor's front yard in circles, just like they do in your yard.

The neighbor comes over to tell you that your kids rode over his freshly cut grass leaving circles. He is upset since he spent two hours mowing and edging his lawn because they are having guests over. You just finished arguing again with your spouse, so you are aggravated that the neighbor has come over to complain. You tell him that "kids will be kids" and that it's "just grass"—no apologies, no telling the children to apologize either. Your neighbor is incensed.

Your negative attitude and energy have just created a neighbor problem.

EXAMPLE

You work long hours and sleep very little. Next door, a teen boy and his friends are playing basketball at midnight on Monday. The boy and his friends play late several nights in a row. You have had a contentious relationship with the parents of this boy over loud music, basketball playing at all hours, cars blocking your driveway, and on and on. Both you and the neighbors hate each other after several nasty conversations.

This toxic relationship affects both your yard and the neighbor's yard. The negative energy will continue to grow and expand causing more nastiness.

In both of these examples, behavior and comments have been affected by negative energy. This causes stress to develop for those living on both sides of this equation. Relations between both sets of neighbors worsen and become glacial. Until this energy is cleared away, apologies will not be made and everyone affected will continue in this negative pattern.

If the energy in your home is very negative, then you should clear it right away. When you pay for massages, energy-healing sessions, or counseling sessions, you feel great in the car until you get home. Walking into the negative energy in your home will counteract all the physical or emotional healing that you just paid for. It drains you and your vibrations.

Your home is suppose to be your sacred space. It is suppose to be warm, loving, and peaceful, so that you may renew yourself and relax. Do not allow your sacred space to be corrupted or adversely impacted by negativity.

Your yard is supposed to be an oasis of peace and pleasure. You, your family, and your friends want to enjoy the pool, garden, or hammock. Allow the positive, sacred energy of your home to flow into your yard instead of the negativity.

Your home and yard should be a welcoming, peaceful place for you to enjoy your life, your family, and your pets. Fill your home with love and light for the purest vibrations.

What's Your Energy?

To assist you in determining whether or not your home and yard's energy is contributing negatively to your life, ask yourself the following questions. Space has been provided for you to write your answers.

1. How do you feel about your home and yard right now?

_____

_____

_____

2. Does being inside your home affect you in a positive or negative manner?

_____

_____

_____

3. What types of activities happen in your home?

_____

_____

_____

4. What types of activities happen in your yard?

_____

_____

_____

5. Do you enjoy living in your neighborhood?

_____

_____

_____

6. Do you get along with your neighbors? If not, why not?

_____

_____

_____

7. What actions will be required by either you or your neighbor to resolve these issues?

_____

_____

_____

8. Describe how your feelings about your home and yard impact your life right now in a positive or negative manner.

_____

_____

_____

CHAPTER 5

THE FIFTH VARIANT = YOUR WORK

Many people have to work to pay their bills and take care of their families. Most people enjoy their careers—they love what they do and have great success. However, some people may like what they do but NOT who they work with. Others will like the people they work with but not the job itself. Everyone needs money. It pays the bills and provides comfortable things in your life. Most people spend the bulk of their day working eight to twelve hours. That is a large part of a life spent in one place. Of course, your workplace will affect your energy.

Sometimes you sit in the parking lot reminding yourself that money pays for your mortgage, car loan, and groceries for your family, so you force yourself to walk into work. Maybe you have to grin and bear it while working with a toxic person. This person may be your boss or your coworker, and they have no plans to leave to make your life easier. You vent on the way home or dump the day's horrible events onto your family and friends.

THE FIFTH VARIANT = YOUR WORK

Monster Boss	Catty Coworker	Location	WORK

Since you spend more time at your workplace than you do at your home, this negativity will affect your production, your attitude, and your physical health. It is not a pleasant sensation to be miserable all of the time when you are trying to make a living.

Here are some examples of how work can affect you.

The Monster Boss

Some people win the lottery and have a great boss. Great bosses are encouraging and assist you to excel. Then there is the Monster Boss. Monster bosses will scream, belittle, criticize, and make life miserable for anyone stuck working for them. This type of boss is very toxic and extremely hard to deal with on a daily basis.

Every morning, you meet with your Monster Boss. He reviews the activities and reports that he requires from you. He advised you to complete a report a certain way "ABC" and that he needs it immediately. You take notes and go off to start your day. When you finish the report in the "ABC" way, you bring it to him. The Monster Boss reviews the report with you standing there. He begins to scream that you did not complete the report in "XYZ" way and that you are incompetent, and he is not sure why he allows you to stay. He rages at you when you pipe up to say he specifically requested "ABC" way. You run back to your desk in tears or frustration to revise the report in the "XYZ" way and frantically rush to complete it. When you once again approach the Monster Boss, he reviews it "XYZ" way and then says it is satisfactory, but you took way too long to get it right. He tells you to go finish the rest of your work. He does not apologize.

This type of boss will never be happy with your work performance, attitude, or abilities. You will constantly be on edge wonderingwhat will upset him next. This is not a healthy place to work, nor is it healthy for your state of mind. You do not deserve this type of treatment. You are not stupid, inefficient, or a bad worker. You just have a Monster Boss.

If you are in this situation, I urge you to clear the energy while you find another job.

Catty Coworker

This type of coworker is underhanded, gossipy, and sly. They will make rude comments on your appearance, how you speak, and how your perform your duties. The catty coworker will steal your ideas, take credit for your work or reporting, and make disparaging remarks about your performance. Sometimes they even blame you for their inefficiencies or deflect their problems onto you. Sabotage is their greatest ability.

Your coworker Cathy is very smug, plus she's sneaky. You are in the coffee room with your friend before the staff meeting. You are excitedly telling your friend about the great idea you had and give her some highlights prior to the meeting. Unbeknownst to you, Cathy was lurking in the hallway and heard every word. When you enter the staff meeting, the boss runs down his agenda and comes to the point where he asks for new ideas. Before you can even raise your hand, Cathy states she has one and begins to list highlights of your "idea." The boss raves to her how wonderful this idea is and asks her to flesh it out. You sit there stunned and look across the table at your friend. You were just sabotaged and had your idea stolen.

Unfortunately, this happens quite often in the workplace. A toxic coworker can make your workplace unbearable. They cause problems within teams and across departments. Sometimes a weak boss will not deal properly with the toxic employee. Their behavior causes undue stress and unpleasantness at the workplace.

Location of Building

Your office or other building is an inanimate object, but it does contain energy. The energy of the location contains the energy of what has happened in the past on the property and the energy of what you and your coworkers are creating in it. This energy in your workplace can make you more depressed, stressed, or unhappy.

You work for a great boss and have an easy relationship with your coworkers. Your company went through a growth spurt and needs a larger building. The executive team searches and finds a new location. Plans are made for the move. Everyone is excited to have more space and more parking.

After the move, some team members begin bickering with each other, and bosses have become short-tempered and demanding. Everyone wonders why no one is getting along now. Clients only stay a short while and leave. No one wants to stay late to work. The negative energy of the place creeps into the energy of those who work in the building and into those who visit it.

One coworker comes across information that a shooting took place in the building when a previous company had rented it. That energy remains inside the building. When he shares the information, everyone freaks out.

The negative energy inside the building or on the property will continue to grow until it is cleared out. A property's energy is affected by what was there before, what has happened on it, and by those who live or work on the property.

When others act in a disrespectful and unprofessional manner, it will impact you negatively. You deserve to work in a safe, professional environment. You treat people at work kindly and in a professional manner. You deserve the same treatment.

If your workplace is unbearable due to toxic people, it is best to clear the energy as swiftly as possible. This energy not only affects you personally, but it will affect the production level of all the people working there. If your boss or coworkers do not change their behavior, then start looking for another job. Finding another job will ensure that you can be less stressed out and stuck in such negativity.

Many people dislike starting a job search. What is the lesser evil to you—job search or staying with toxic coworkers? That is a decision you will have to make. In the Appendix, I have listed an exercise to bring positive energy into your job search.

What's Your Energy?

To assist you in determining whether or not your workplace's energy is contributing negatively to your life, ask yourself the following questions. Space has been provided for you to write your answers.

1. How do you feel about your workplace right now?

_____

_____

_____

_____

_____

_____

2. Does being at work affect you in a positive or negative manner?

_____

_____

_____

3. Which type of boss do you have? Do you like him or her?

_____

_____

_____

4. Do you feel supported by your boss?

_____

_____

_____

5. Do you get along with your coworkers? If not, why not?

_____

_____

_____

6. In which ways do your coworkers assist you or sabotage you?

_____

_____

_____

7. Do you get upset or aggravated when you simply walk into your building?

_____

_____

_____

8. Describe how your feelings about your workplace impact your life right now in a positive or negative manner.

_____

_____

_____

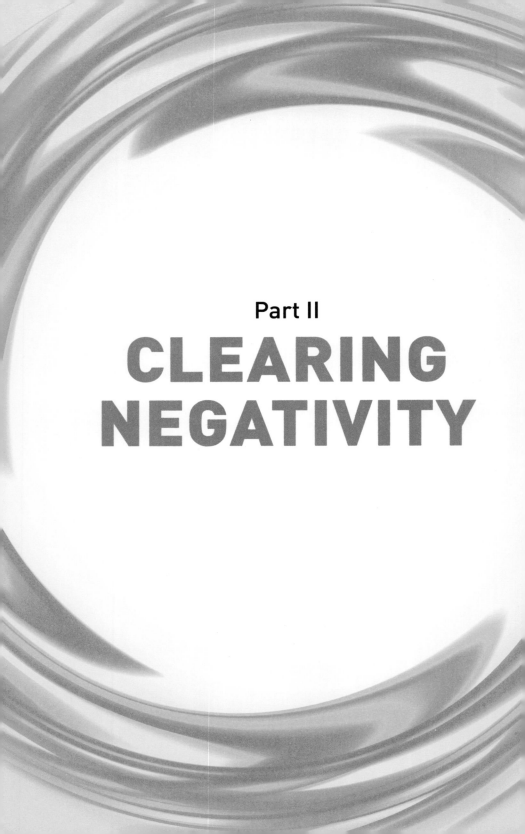

Part II

CLEARING NEGATIVITY

CHAPTER 6

TOOLS IN YOUR HOME OR GROCERY STORE

How You Can Combat Negative Energy In Your Everyday Life

The tools you will require are very simple and can be found in your house, garden, grocery store, or local new age or religious shop. I am going to tell you about the tools and then explain how to use each of them. These tools have been proven to work over and over by my own use, my clients' use, and by those that have attended my workshops.

Are you ready to clear the negativity from your life? Are you ready to get positive and to live positive? Here is the first set of tools.

Lemon—Nature's Cleanser

Manufacturers use lemon oil and lemon juice in multiple products that are used to clean your car, home, office, and other locations. You too

TOOLS IN YOUR HOME OR GROCERY STORE

LEMON

LEMON JUICE

SEA SALT

may use the power of this natural cleanser to cleanse the energy between you and someone else. No, you do not throw a lemon at them! If you are dealing with an extremely toxic or nasty person, lemon juice is a wonderful tool to use.

The Lemon Process
1. Write the toxic or nasty person's name on piece of paper.
2. Place the paper on a piece of aluminum foil.
3. Next, saturate the paper with lemon juice from a slice of lemon (or you may use bottled lemon juice).
4. Close the foil around the paper and place in your freezer.

You may write several names on the same paper, or place the paper in a whole lemon. Either way, this begins to work immediately. It does not matter what color paper that you use, nor does it matter if you use pen, pencil, crayon, or even eyeliner.

Why does this work? It works because you are using lemon juice to cleanse the energy between you. You are completing an action of protection and clearing to remove their negative energy or toxicity from your being. When you place their name in the freezer, you are saying "no more" to their negative actions.

You may leave the paper in the freezer until you notice a change in attitude or the behavior of the toxic person(s). Sometimes it may only be days; other people require weeks.

Afterwards, you may just throw the "lemonized" paper away. For super toxic people, you may have to repeat this exercise a few more times. Each time you do this, it will lessen their negativity towards you.

Sea Salt

Sea salt is an earth mineral and is very beneficial to you. You may use it in a variety of ways to remove negativity. Sea salts are harvested from the Atlantic, Pacific, and Indian Oceans and from the Caribbean, Celtic, and Dead Seas. It does not matter which kind of sea salt you use. You may use either coarse or fine-grade salts. Iodized salt has been chemically treated and should not be used for this exercise.

Bathing

People have gone to the sea to bathe for centuries. Swimming and bathing in sea salt relaxes your muscles and heals small abrasions and cuts. As you go through your day, you pick up mucky energy from the various locations and people you meet. This energy affects your aura and emotional energies.

1. To clear this muck off of you, fill a bath tub with the hottest water that you can handle.
2. Pour sea salt into your hand, filling your palm.
3. Empty your hand of salt into the water and soak in the bath for at least twenty minutes.

The sea salt will work on your body and muscles to minimize stress, and it will pull off any negativity that you have absorbed throughout your day. You should try to bathe in sea salt at least once a week. You may bathe more often if you live with or work with toxic people.

If you prefer not to bathe but would rather shower, purchase a sea salt shaker and pour the salt on your washcloth or loofah sponge.

Cooking

People use spices in various dishes as they cook. By using sea salt to flavor your foods, you are ingesting a little bit of positive energy. Sea salt has a wonderful vibration that will enhance your body's natural vibration.

Your emotions while you are preparing and cooking food do affect the energy of the food. If you are angry or upset while chopping, dicing, and cooking, that anger will energize the food. Your positive state of mind of being happy or in a good mood will also energize the food. Cooking with love is always a higher vibration and is a better way to ensure no negativity is consumed.

Clearing Negative Energy from the Perimeter of Your Home

Sprinkle the sea salt outside the perimeter of your home, especially under doors or windows. This will remove any negative energy that is inside your home. You may also sprinkle the sea salt along your property line to remove any stagnant energy from your yard. However, if you use too much of the salt, it will burn your grass, trees, bushes, or flowers. Make sure you spread it lightly.

You may also use sea salt at other locations, like your office building, store, restaurant, farm, or other types of businesses. It will remove any negative energy from these locations. You should make a sea salt grid of your property line and home at least four times a year. You may do so more often if you live with toxic people.

> Note: Another alternative for you home and yard's energy, Cosmic Dust, may be found in Chapter 8.

Case Studies: Using Lemon Juice

I present many classes and workshops at expos, conferences, stores, and online webinars. Many people are shocked when I hold up a lemon during my "Clearing the Negativity" class. When I explain how to use lemon juice, there are many "oohs" and "ahhs" from the attendees. Here are the results of some case studies.

My husband and I are now retired and spend more time together. However, he can be occasionally very grumpy. This grumpiness tends to last for a few days and makes life very unpleasant. He will begin to complain about everything I do from my cooking to my cleaning. After I attended your class, he began one of his grumpy moods. He started in at me about breakfast (I didn't make enough bacon!) and then it progressed. He finally descended to his workroom in the basement. I just couldn't deal with another continued grumpy streak. I remembered your tip about the lemon, so I wrote his name, squeezed my lemon bottle on the paper, and stuck his name in the freezer. Thirty minutes later he came upstairs and apologized to me! He said he was sorry for being so disagreeable and gave me a kiss!

Sandy, New York

I work with a small team for a great firm. We get along well. One of the employees retired and the firm hired someone new. The new guy, Bob, started out nicely. About one month after his start date, he began to make criticisms of one team member, then another, and so on. He was very passive-aggressive about his comments. Bob would say things in the nicest-sounding way, but the comments were not very nice. He began to cause much friction in our team.

After attending your workshop, I lemon-juiced his name and froze it. The next day was the first day that he did not make one of his criticisms. That week was a good one for our team. We were back to getting along, and Bob's attitude was so much better. Every now and then he starts up again, so I lemon-juice him when I get home. It works every time!

Kevin, Ohio

CHAPTER 7

TOOLS IN YOUR GARDEN

The next set of tools may be found already growing in your garden or at your local garden center. These tools are plants and herbs, which are very beneficial to clearing negativity and stress from your life.

Sage

Burning sage is an ancient custom and is used in many religious and shamanic practices. Sage clears negative energy from any location and promotes positive vibrations. The best types of sage to use in this exercise are known as White Sage or Desert Sage.

If you are already growing sage in your garden:
1. Cut some stems and hang them in a cool, dry place for five days. This allows the sage to dry out.
2. When the sage is dry and crackly, gather together and tie with twine, thread, or ribbon to create a small bundle or smudge stick.

TOOLS IN YOUR GARDEN

SAGE

LAVENDER

LEMON BALM

3. Grab your smudge stick or sage bundle , a lighter, and a flat dish or shell to begin.

4. Light your smudge so that it begins to smoke.

5. As the sage smokes, you will walk throughout your home or other location room by room saying, "I am clearing all negative energy from my home. Only positive energy remains." It is important that you pay special attention to corners of rooms and all doorways.

6. Make sure you complete this on every livable floor of a residence. Sometimes, the smudge will need to be re-lit, so carry the lighter with you.

It does not matter which room you start with. Some people prefer the kitchen as the "heart of the home," and others prefer starting at the front door. You do not have to clear crawl spaces or unlived-in attics. If your garage is attached to your home, also walk the length of the garage to clear its space.

You should sage your home a minimum of four times per year. You may sage more often depending on the energy of your home.

> **Note:** You should not burn freshly cut sage.

Lavender

The use of lavender has been documented for centuries. It has been used for medicines, aromatherapy, and magical purposes. Lavender assists in calming people down and bringing peace into homes. Aromatherapy uses include reducing headaches and anxiety. Lavender may also be used for attracting love and inducing dreams.

For this exercise, lavender will be used for its purification of energy.

1. Cut lavender stems from your plant and hang them in a cool, dry place for five days. This allows the lavender to dry out.
2. When the lavender is dry and crackly, gather together and tie with twine, thread, or ribbon to create a small bundle or smudge stick.
3. As the lavender smokes, you will walk throughout your home or other location room by room saying, "I am clearing all negative energy from my home. Only positive energy remains."

You may wish to bundle both the lavender and sage together for this purpose. Combined, they make a wonderful energy smudge.

Lemon Balm

Lemon balm is a plant that has been used for medicines, aromatherapy, and magical purposes. It will assist you in emotional healing. It also relieves stress. Lemon balm's magical properties are for attracting love and deepening physical pleasure.

To use lemon balm, brew it like a tea or add it to your tea mix. Drinking it like tea or in your tea will relieve headaches, calms nerves, and relieves stress. You may also use it as an herb for a light lemon flavoring in foods.

Use it in your bath for emotional healing. By healing your emotions, you will be more open to love. Magical properties of bathing in lemon balm state it will attract love into your life. If you are already in a relationship, bathing in lemon balm helps to deepen physical pleasure with your lover.

You may also dry some of the stems and burn them like sage in your bedroom.

Case Studies: Sage, Lavender, and Lemon Balm

One of my webinar attendees was Marianne. She had asked about relieving emotional stress saying that she experienced an overabundance of emotions during the month and wanted something natural to use. I suggested that she add fresh lavender and lemon balm to her bath. She stated:

Your suggestion to use lavender and lemon balm is really helping me. I have a lavender plant and found lemon balm to plant. I love the smell of them when I am soaking in the tub. It is very peaceful to lay in the water with lavender flowers and lemon balm leaves. I soak for twenty-five minutes before bathing. My soul feels so refreshed and I am crying a lot less. I also began drying both of these plants and using them in my herbal teas. This has made such a difference for me. Thank you!

Marianne, Virginia

Jessica attended one of my classes and was already using sage. However, she complained that sometimes the sage smoke was not a pleasant smell when she smudged. She also said she felt she needed more calming energy since she had young children. I suggested to her to add some dried lavender to her smudge to increase the calming effect of her energy clearing and to enhance the smell.

Adding the lavender made such a difference! It was not at all hard to add the lavender sprigs to my sage smudge. I just pushed the lavender stems into the middle of the sage and a couple of other spots like you said. The sage smells sweeter with the lavender. I also added a little vase of lavender in my bedroom. My house feels "better"; I don't know how it works but it does. The kids are calmer, my dog is calmer, my husband is calmer, and so am I. I am less aggravated so I'm going to keep using the lavender with those smudge sticks.

Jessica, Pennsylvania

CHAPTER 8

TOOLS IN YOUR METAPHYSICAL STORE

The following tools may be found in your local metaphysical, new age, religious, pagan, or Wiccan shop. Their prices vary by area. You may also pick up some of these items at local metaphysical expos or fairs that showcase vendors. Most store owners or expo vendors will be able to provide you various sizes or additional information on using these tools.

Copal Resin Incense

Copal is an incense resin that is black or white in color. Ancient people burned copal in their rituals. This resin is a very earthy-smelling scent and is quite powerful. You may create your own ritual of cleansing the energy in your home with this wonderful resin incense.

1. You will need a small metal bowl, sea salt (or sand), and incense charcoal. Please note that copal will not melt in your potpourri burners.

TOOLS IN YOUR METAPHYSICAL STORE

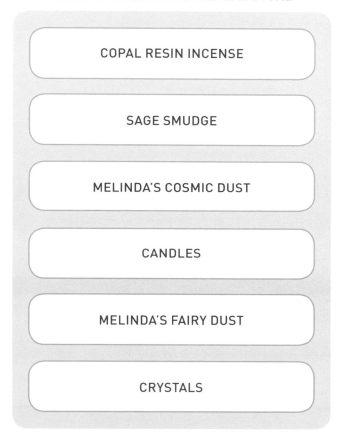

COPAL RESIN INCENSE

SAGE SMUDGE

MELINDA'S COSMIC DUST

CANDLES

MELINDA'S FAIRY DUST

CRYSTALS

2. Fill the bottom of your metal bowl with sea salt or sand and place the round incense charcoal on the salt/sand.
3. Next, you will light the charcoal. Wait for the charcoal to glow orange.
4. Drop one or two pieces of the copal resin onto the charcoal. The copal will begin to smoke.
5. As the resin smokes, you will walk through out your home or other location, room by room, ssaying, "I am clearing all negative energy from my home. Only positive energy remains."

It is important that you pay special attention to corners of rooms and all doorways. Make sure you complete this on every livable floor of a residence.

It does not matter which room you start with. Some people prefer the kitchen as the "heart of the home" and others prefer starting at the front door. You do not have to clear crawl spaces or unlived-in attics. If your garage is attached to your home, also walk the length of the garage to clear its space also.

You should clear the energy or your home or other location with the Copal at least four times per year.

Sage Bundle or Smudge Stick

For those of you without a garden, you may purchase a sage smudge stick from your local metaphysical store. Refer to chapter 7 for more information on the use of sage to clear negativity.

Melinda's Cosmic Dust™

Cosmic Dust removes and then blocks negative energy from your home or other location. My creation of this product is referenced in the Preface. This proprietary recipe is an energy-charged mix. It is a great alternative to sage. Many people have asthma or other breathing disorders and cannot handle the sage smoke.

To use the Cosmic Dust:

1. Pinch a small amount from the bag with your fingers.
2. Sprinkle it at the four corners of your property line. Since it is energy-charged, it will make an energy grid from the four corners of your property. This clears any negative energy found in your yard.
3. Next, sprinkle it on the four corners of your house.

The Cosmic Dust will make an energy grid around your home to remove and block negative energy from your home.

Since you are only using a small amount at each of the four corners, your grass, trees, bushes, or flowers will not be affected.

You may also use the Cosmic Dust inside your home for truly toxic situations. If you regularly argue or have petty disagreements with your spouse, children, or other family members, sprinkle it in the four corners of that person's bedroom. This will help remove their negativity. For those of you who do not like "dust" in the corners of any room, allow the Cosmic Dust to sit for at least thirty minutes to clear the energy. You may then vacuum it up.

Another way to use the Cosmic Dust is at your workplace. Your boss or coworkers may not allow or appreciate you walking in with a burning sage stick.

Perform the following steps with Cosmic Dust at your work.

1. Pinch a small amount of the Cosmic Dust with your fingers.
2. Sprinkle it in the four corners of your office, cubicle, or pod. Make sure you flick a little bit in the doorway. This will clear the energy of your work space.

Do you work with a Monster Boss or Catty Coworker? You can use the Cosmic Dust to cleanse their energy and attitude toward you. Flick a small amount of the dust either on the seat or under the chair of the person (boss or coworker) causing problems.

You should use Cosmic Dust in your home or other location a minimum of four times per year. You may clear the energy more often depending on the energy of your home or other location.

Candles

Candles are a great tool to clear energy or to raise the vibrations of any home or location. It is best to clear your home first with sage, copal, or Cosmic Dust prior to raising the energy vibrations.

You may purchase name brand candles like Crystal Journey or Coventry Creations that make their own "positive energy" candles. If you are on a budget, purchase colored candles.

Religious stores sell tall, seven-day candles with various Christian, Buddhist, Santeria, or other icons on them. Choose your favorite god, goddess, or saint candle and light it once to clear the energy from your home.

You may also choose a plain yellow or white candle to light. Yellow is the color of sunshine and positive energy, and white is the color of the universe.

You can increase the positive energy by pouring sea salt into the bottom of the candle holder. The sea salt boosts the candle's energy. You may also place your favorite crystal next to the candle. Please note you should always keep an eye on any open flame in your home.

Light a candle anytime that you feel the need to increase the positive energy in your home.

Melinda's Fairy Dust™

Melinda's Fairy Dust raises the energy vibrations inside your home or other location. It increases the level of joy and happiness energy. My creation of this product is referenced in the Preface. This proprietary recipe is an energy-charged mix.

To use the Fairy Dust:

1. Pinch a small amount from the bag with your fingers.
2. Sprinkle it at the four corners of your property line. Since it is energy-charged, it will make an energy grid from the four corners of your property. This raises the energy vibrations found in your yard.
3. Next, sprinkle it on the four corners of your house. The Fairy Dust will make an energy grid around your home to increase positive energy for your home.

Since you are only using a small amount at each of the four corners, your grass, trees, bushes, or flowers will not be affected.

You may also use the Fairy Dust inside your home. Sprinkle a small amount around your dining area to increase good vibrations for happy dining experiences. This is especially great for family holiday dinners! You may also sprinkle a pinch in your meditation or yoga rooms. It will increase the vibrations for your sessions.

In the bedroom, flick a small amount in the four corners or under the four corners of your bed. The joy and happiness energy will assist you in your personal relationships. For those of you who do not like "dust" in the corners of any room, allow the Cosmic Dust to sit for at least thirty minutes to clear the energy. You may then vacuum it up.

At work, pinch a small amount of the Fairy Dust with your fingers, and sprinkle it in the four corners of your office, cubicle, or pod. Make sure you flick a little bit in the doorway. This will raise positive energy in your work space.

If you own a store, restaurant, or other business, flick a small pinch into your cash register or tip jars to increase the positive energy. The Fairy Dust will attract "more" into that location.

You should use Fairy Dust in your home or other location a minimum of four times per year. You may raise the energy more often depending on the energy of your home or other location.

Crystals

Crystals are energy conductors. They receive and send energy. Crystals are great to use both to clear negative energy and to raise positive energy for your physical self, aura, or space. There are hundreds of crystals to choose from. I am going to review the four crystals that everyone should have—these are the building blocks you should begin with.

Clear Quartz

Clear Quartz is an all-in-one power crystal. This is the first crystal that you should buy. It absorbs negative energy from any location. It also boosts the power of other crystals and offers healing energy.

To use Clear Quartz, place a large piece in each hand. The crystals will allow energy to flow through your body. You should concentrate on which emotions or what events you want to release from your being. You may either sit quietly or meditate for at least ten minutes with the Clear Quartz in your hands.

Clear Quartz may also be placed in any room in your house to absorb negative energy or emotions. Make sure you place a piece next to your computer or laptop to absorb energies from the internet. Periodically, give the crystals a sea salt bath or run them under running water to clear any negative energy.

Rose Quartz

Rose Quartz is a pink-colored crystal with vast healing properties. It removes emotional debris from your Heart Chakra. It also releases negative thoughts and low self-esteem. It will also attract love into your life.

To use a Rose Quartz, hold it in the center of both of your hands. You should concentrate on which emotions or events that you want to release from your being. You may either sit quietly, pray, or meditate for at least ten minutes with the Rose Quartz in your hands.

You may also place a piece of Rose Quartz on your heart while you are laying down. This allows emotional healing of your Heart Chakra. You may sit quietly, pray, or meditate for at least ten minutes. Ladies, you may also place a piece in your bra for emotional healing.

If you are having surgery or physical issues, lay a piece of Rose Quartz on your bed or nightstand. Place four pieces in the corners of your bedroom or under your bed to make a peaceful, loving energy grid. This grid will open you to love or deepen current relationships.

Amethyst

Amethyst is a high-vibration, healing crystal. It carries the vibrations of both red crystals (for love) and blue crystals (for power). It brings peace to your state of mind. It will also deepen your spiritual connection while meditating or channeling.

To use Amethyst, you need eight pieces to create a grid. These can be small, medium, or large pieces. Lie on the floor or on your bed, whichever is most comfortable for you. Next, surround yourself with the crystals. Place one above your head, one by your feet, one at each shoulder, and one at each side of your waist and knees. You've just created an Amethyst grid that will energetically connect to each crystal. Lay quietly; pray or meditate for twenty minutes in the Amethyst grid. You do not have to buy an expensive Amethyst bed to experience healing!

Selenite

Selenite is the White Light crystal. It brings the White Light into any location. It is also a peaceful crystal. Selenite's powerful vibration assists you to open yourself to higher consciousness. It connects to your higher self (soul) allowing access to your past or future lives.

To use Selenite, hold a piece in your hand while running it up and down your Chakra points to clear them. It will help to pull negative energy from your physical and emotional being. It will also remove negativity from your aura.

You may also place Selenite in any room to bring peace and remove tension. It can be used to clear energy of other stones. Selenite should not be placed in water because it will dissolve. You do not have to clear the energy of this crystal; it will cleanse itself.

Special Note: When purchasing crystals, clean them first with a mixture of sea salt and water (let them soak at least fifteen minutes), shake them in a bag of sea salt, or rinse them under running water. Let them air dry. You should cleanse your crystals a minimum of four times per year. Cleanse their energy more often if you use them a lot or if you live with toxic people. As mentioned, never place Selenite into water; it will dissolve.

There are many other crystals that can be used for various aspects or issues. Please obtain a crystal book from your local library or book store to review other crystals and their uses.

Case Studies: Clearing Home & Yard Energy

During the question and answer session of one of my webinars, Carol asked me about resolving an issue with one of her neighbors. She used to be friendly with her neighbor down the street until the woman began gossiping about her and attempting to wreck her friendship with another neighbor. I recommended that she clear and protect her yard by using my Cosmic Dust and Fairy Dust. I also recommended that she place Clear Quartz crystals in the four corners of her yard. Here are Carol's results:

As you suggested, I buried 4 crystals into the 4 corners of my yard. I also sprinkled the Cosmic Dust at each corner and your Fairy Dust by my front and back doors. Later that afternoon, I was dusting my living room and saw my problem neighbor Diana walking her dogs on the sidewalk up the street towards my house. Imagine my surprise when she got to my neighbor's house, she and her dogs walked into the street. She stayed in the street until she got to my other neighbor's house and then returned to the sidewalk. She could not walk on my sidewalk! The Cosmic Dust and Clear Quartz blocked her negative self! This happened each day that she walked that week. She could not come onto my property. Thank you Melinda for your advice!

Carol, California

At one store, I presented my "Clearing the Negativity" class. Linda was an attendee that evening and approached me afterwards to discuss protecting her home's energy and to raise the vibrations. She was interested in having a more natural, peaceful feeling in her home. I recommended that she use a sage smudge and my Cosmic Dust to clear the energy, and to use my Fairy Dust to raise the vibrations of her home. Here are Linda's results from clearing and raising the vibrations of her home and yard:

I would like to tell you a story of magic, miracle, love, and goodness. I bought Melinda's Cosmic Dust and Fairy Dust a couple months ago. I walked my property and sprinkled little bits of Cosmic Dust on the corners of the property. I spoke prayers of love and protection while walking. I invited loving, kind, protection to bless my home and grounds. I also went around my physical house and sprinkled dust at all the corners and edges, wherever I felt I should go. I spoke love and gratitude for my home and blessings, my life, my son, and all who enter my doors and realm. I requested that any unwanted energy leave my little paradise. I was filled with wonder, awe, love, and peace. Such a wonderful feeling! I especially sprinkled a little extra at the doors around the house to boost the entryways and exits.

Then, I took the Fairy Dust and welcomed the magic and wonder of the fairy kingdom to bless me with joy and happiness, health, and well being. I also sprinkled some on all my window sills, upstairs and downstairs, and in places where I felt it would be welcomed.

Then the unspeakable happened in my neighborhood. About a month later, I got a call from my next door neighbor who informed me they were robbed and vandalized. Not only them, but the neighbor on the *other* side of me, too! My heart was pounding and I felt faint, but not from fear. I felt compassion and concern for my neighbors. I knew *instantly* why and how I was protected. Why and how was it that they passed me by? We were right there, not far away. We live in the country, but the neighbors are close. I will tell you how and why. The magical and loving Cosmic Dust and Fairy Dust, along with my pure and genuine prayers, saved me from that horrible possibility.

While I felt relief they passed me by, I felt sorrow for my neighbors and their loss. There were valuable and sentimental items stolen, not to mention the damage to the house and the emotional pain. Less than a week later, my neighbor called and told me the criminals were apprehended and were put behind bars.

While I didn't feel comfortable telling my neighbor about my *spiritual* protection, I surely reinforced a couple days later what I originally sprinkled that month ago. I put some polite sprinkles on the edge of *their* property too, while sending my prayers for their protection and the entire community. I also burned some white sage everywhere in the house and around it as well, for cleansing. I hope someday I will feel moved to tell the neighbors. Sometimes you have to wait for when the moment is right.

I am so grateful for Melinda's magical dust! When people come over they *always* remark what a lovely, peaceful, endearing house I live in and land I dwell on.

Linda, Ohio

Case Studies: Clearing Work Issues

I presented my "Clearing the Negativity" lecture at the State of the Art (astrology) conference in Buffalo, New York. One of the attendees, Jim, approached me afterwards with questions relating to his workplace. Jim works at a City office in New York. They were having many issues, and there was much fear about upcoming changes. I recommended that he attempt an energy clearing at his workplace with my Cosmic Dust and Fairy Dust since he could not use a sage smudge. Here are Jim's results from clearing the energy at work:

I had purchased several packets of your Fairy and Cosmic Dusts at the SOTA conference in 2010. Shortly after returning home to my day job as a municipal employee, there was a municipal election where a generally dissatisfied electorate voted the majority of the previous council out of office.

Needless to say, there was a lot of negative energy in the air and fear among those who provide the day-to-day services. I used my entire stock around the offices. I shouldn't have been surprised, but after a short period of apprehension between the new council and staff, things settled down to a positive and constructive relationship. As you said, the dusts have a good life, as I sense they are still at work today.

Jim, New York

After I presented my workshop at a metaphysical expo in Ohio, an attendee, Kathy, approached me about her boss. She was experiencing a very aggressive boss whose mood swings quickly alternated between happy, aggravated, and angry. I recommended that she sprinkle a little Cosmic Dust in her office and on her supervisor's chair. Here are Kathy's results at work:

I wanted you to know again how much I enjoyed your workshop and the ideas that you shared. I did put the Cosmic Dust on both seats that my supervisor sits on. She seems to have changed her attitude and we get along now and laugh more often. It is a whole new atmosphere. Thank you for your Fairy Dust and the Cosmic Dust.

Kathy, Ohio

CHAPTER 9

TOOLS THAT ARE FREE

The following tools are absolutely free. You can begin right now, today, to use these tools to remove negative energy from your body, your relationships, your home, or your workplace. I recommend that you use these free tools in combination with the other inexpensive tools listed in the previous chapters.

Colors

Colors are an important component of our lives. We are surrounded by colors in our clothing, homes, work places, and stores. Not only do we respond in a visual way to colors, we also respond in an energetic way to them. We are physically made of energy and, in kind, respond to other energy forces.

You may use color to change your attitude or mood via clothing, as an accent in your home décor, or in your workplace. You may also

TOOLS THAT ARE FREE

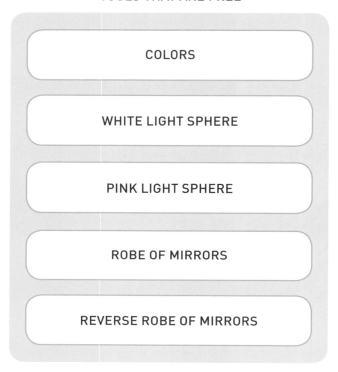

COLORS

WHITE LIGHT SPHERE

PINK LIGHT SPHERE

ROBE OF MIRRORS

REVERSE ROBE OF MIRRORS

visualize a ball of color around yourself or someone else to change the physical energy of a person. The last way to use color is with candle magic—burning specific colors of candles to obtain energy changes.

Here is a guide to colors and how to use them to change your energy.

Red

Red is the color of love, passion, and self-esteem. Use this color when you have a lack of energy or you are feeling insecure. Red boosts self-esteem and makes you feel stronger. It also attracts the eye of others and draws love into your life. It is the color of fire and brings a hot energy into your life. Red is also the color of your Root Chakra.

Orange

Orange is a vibrant energy and should be used when you feel bleak or if you feel blocked by something in your life. It will motivate you to make a change or make a move to become unstuck. It is a color of fire and brings a warmer energy into your life. Orange is also the color of your Sacral Chakra.

Yellow

Yellow is the color of sunshine and happiness. Use this color when you feel lethargic or suffer from anxiety or panic attacks. It will reduce anxiety and stress, bringing a warm energy into your life. Yellow is the color of your Solar Plexus Chakra.

Green

Green is the color of calmness, abundance, and fertility. Use this color when you need a new state of balance or calmness in your life. You may also use it for Law of Attraction work to allow abundance and prosperity into your life. Green also works in fertility rituals or for creativity. It will bring a cooling energy into your life. Green is the color of your Heart Chakra.

Blue

Blue is a power color that draws command of others, brings assertiveness, and helps the easy flow of communication. Use this color when you need to speak in front of groups or at work for presentations. It is a color that inspires trust and loyalty. This color will also bring a cool energy into your life. Blue is the color of your Throat Chakra.

Violet

Violet is a color that charges your intuition and gives you the ability to see what is hidden. It also is a calming color for stress. Use Violet during any psychic development classes or when you need to rebalance your life. It is the energy of tepid heat. Violet is the color of your Third Eye Chakra.

Indigo

Indigo is the color to deepen your connection to the Divine and to assist you with meditation. Indigo helps provide the needed space and solitude to renew your energy. This is the color of warm power. Indigo is the color of your Crown Chakra.

Turquoise

Turquoise is the color for emotional and physical healing. Turquoise promotes mental health and also strengthens inner confidence. Use this color to boost your self-esteem during sickness or stress. Turquoise has a cool energy.

Pink

Pink is the color of love, friendship, and healing. Pink calms moods and attitudes while reducing tension. Use this color to strengthen relationship bonds in all situations. It will also calm people and reduce stress. Pink may also be used for emotional healing. Pink is a warm energy.

Brown

Brown is the color of the Earth and grounding energy. It will bring stability to any atmosphere while strengthening connections between people. Use this color to have conversations with people with whom you have difficult relationships. Brown is also great to use to ground your energy and for rituals connecting you to Mother Earth. This color has a neutral energy.

Gray

Gray is a power color. It is the color of diplomacy and peace. Use gray to boost the power of any of the colors mentioned above. You may use this color for obtaining qualities of peace in situations. Gray will also stabilize relationships. This color has a neutral energy.

Black

Black is the color of protection, concealment, and energy absorption. Use this color when you require energetic protection from others or when you need to absorb energy. Black may also be used to conceal your flaws from others. It is the energy of gestation and preparation, so use it if you have writer's block or need help with a creative project. This color has a neutral energy.

White

White is a color that represents fresh starts and new beginnings. It is a color of purity and hope. Use this color whenever you are starting a new relationship, job, or event. This color may also be used when you are looking for hope and faith. It has a neutral energy.

White Light Sphere

Everyone should begin their day by circling themselves in a sphere of the White Light of the Universe or Holy Spirit. This is your first level of psychic protection. It keeps the negative energy of others away from your aura and being. The sphere will also protect you from energy vampires. All you have to say is:

"I circle myself in the White Light of the Universe (or Holy Spirit) for love and protection."

Once you have this layer of White Light surrounding you, you may also add other colors for various purposes.

Pink Light Sphere

When you are going through a difficult time or a crisis, circle yourself in a Sphere of Pink Light. Pink is the color of love and healing. It will reduce your stress and tension and help you to feel better about yourself. Other people will react in a more positive manner toward you when you are surrounded in Pink Light. It draws people to you and reduces tension.

Here is a secret use: Throw a Pink Light Sphere onto someone who causes you stress or is quite toxic. No, you cannot buy a paint gun and splatter them in pink paint! But you can send Pink Light Spheres to other people to make them less toxic or harsh towards you.

Robe of Mirrors

Another great way to protect yourself from toxic or negative people is to use a Robe of Mirrors. No, you do not need to go to the local hardware store and buy mirror squares to glue onto your bathrobe! Instead, visualize a liquid robe of mirrors pouring down from your Crown Chakra to the tips of your toes. The shiny part of the mirror reflects outward from your physical being. It is a psychic protection tool.

The Robe of Mirrors will reflect back to anyone what type of energy they are sending to you. If they are sending blessings to you, then blessings are reflected to them. If they are sending negativity or toxic energy to you, it cannot attach to you or affect you. It will be reflected back to them. This is very effective for dealing with poor working conditions, stressful family members, or any time you feel you need to protect your aura.

Reverse Robe of Mirrors

Just as you may use the Robe of Mirrors to reflect outward from your being to protect yourself, you may also use it to stop the person sending toxic or negative energy in their tracks. Visualize the toxic person in your mind. Then visualize a shiny liquid robe of mirrors encasing the person with the shiny part of the mirror facing the person. This stops their ability to send negative or toxic energy to anyone and reflects back onto them. It is a great psychic protection tool to use. However, the person may break the Reverse Robe of Mirrors at any time.

Case Studies: Colors

Many people forget how colors affect us—from seeing colors in our environment, wearing them in our clothing, to our attitudes throughout the day. Colors are an instant pick-me-up and can assist you with moving your life forward. Here are two wonderful examples.

I am in college and usually wear all black. I had to begin my student teaching and I was crazy nervous. I looked at my notes that I took during your class to see if something would help me. So I borrowed my sister's blue dress for my first day of teaching—blue for speaking in front of others. It was a different kind of energy when I put that dress on. It made me braver. It was a good day with the third grade students. I then went and bought a blue dress of my own and an emerald green shirt (for calmness) to go with my black pants. I thank you for teaching us about colors.

Rhonda, Ohio

You taught us about the Pink Sphere in your class. I decided that when I went out with my girlfriends on Friday to circle in that pink light. I wanted to know if it worked and if guys would approach me. Usually they go talk to my friend first. She's not shy like me.

I felt a little goofy when I said the pink was all around me, but it did feel nicer. That energy you spoke about . . . it was nice. I did have two guys come talk to me that night. One of them I even danced with. We exchanged numbers and I hope to hear from him. So that pink light is something I will try again!

Donna, Kentucky

CHAPTER 10

TOOLS FOR YOUR MIND

Your mind is a very powerful organ. Your thoughts are energy. When you speak those thoughts, they amplify that energy. When you talk to people or speak about yourself in a positive manner, you amplify positive energy. When you talkk to people or speak about yourself in a negative manner, you amplify negative energy.

This creates a pattern for you. You must decide which pattern you want to have—a negative one or a positive one. This energy becomes your thought intention. It reverberates around you. Remember, likes attracts like. Negativity will attract more negative energy. Being positive will attract more positive energy.

You are human, so you have Free Will and the ability to feel a range of emotions. Not only can you experience anger, frustration, anxiety, and fear, you can also feel joy, happiness, contentment, and peace. Not everyone will be like Tiny Tim tiptoeing through the tulips being happy, happy, happy all of the time. But you also do not want to be Debbie Downer or Miserable Matt either!

TOOLS FOR YOUR MIND

POSITIVE THOUGHTS

AFFIRMATIONS

MUSIC

BREAKING HEXES

Think Positive Thoughts

When you are stuck in negative thought patterns, it will affect you energetically. This energy infuses your physical, emotional, and spiritual being. Your thoughts are energy. You control your thoughts; therefore, you are creating the energy around you. It seeps around you and clouds your decision-making process.

Bring positive energy, positive people, and positive events into yourself by BEING POSITIVE. It is that simple.

Change your thought pattern from "I cannot find a good man" to "I have a good man." Stating out loud "I am never lucky" impacts you negatively. Instead, say, "I am surrounded by good luck tonight." What about not wanting to go to a family event or work function? Say out loud, "I am going to have a good time today and meet great people."

Remove the following words from your vocabulary.

- Cannot
- Will not
- Should not
- Have not
- But not
- Do not

These are negative words that bring negative energy into your thoughts and statements. Any time that you think these statements in your head and utter them out loud, you are thinking in a negative pattern. They are self-defeating and sabotaging statements. These words color your energy and lower your vibrations.

Add the following words to your vocabulary.

- I can
- I will
- I have
- I am
- I do

These are positive words that bring positive energy into your thoughts and statements. Using these words enhances your energy and your ability to accomplish your goals and dreams. They will raise your energy vibrations. These words reverberate positively in your energy stream.

Changing your thought patterns is not always easy because you will sabotage yourself by reverting back to old, comfortable, negative patterns. If you catch yourself making a negative statement, say: "cancel, clear," to remove the energy, and re-state using a positive sentence. You can be successful in thinking positively about yourself and your life.

I recommend this exercise to help you in changing your thought patterns. While you are standing in front of a mirror every morning brushing your teeth or your hair, you will state one good, positive thing about yourself. This positive statement may be about your physical appearance, your personality characteristics, or your family or work role. For example:

- I am having a great hair day.
- I have a charming laugh.
- I am a wonderful dad.
- I am an excellent administrative assistant.

You should also say. "I love you" to yourself after every positive statement. Do this for seven straight days.

These statements are very powerful and promote positive thinking and energy. They will support your changing pattern. They will raise your energy vibrations.

If you are not sure that this exercise will work, then write on a sheet of paper how you feel about yourself. Put that paper away for a week. Then begin this exercise to change your thought pattern. After the seventh day, write out how you feel about yourself again. Then grab that first sheet and compare how you felt seven days ago to how you feel today. You will see a difference!

State Positive Affirmations

Stating positive affirmations will raise your energy vibrations and help you to change your thought patterns. By changing your thought patterns, you begin to change your behavior patterns. Affirmations will allow your intentions to be surrounded in positive energy. This allows the Natural Law of Attraction to begin working for you and with you! Remember, your thoughts are energy and speaking amplifies that energy.

I wrote these affirmations and state them daily. I am sharing them with you:

- I act in a positive manner with positive energy flowing into my life in all directions.
- My energy is aligned with the Divine and I flow in love, light, abundance, and positive energy.
- My life is full of positive energy, laughter, gifts, blessings, and joy.
- I am open and worthy of all that the Universe has to offer, and I accept these wonderful gifts now.
- My possibilities are endless: I create them, I see them!

The tone of your voice is very important when stating positive affirmations for your personal or professional goals. You should say these statements in a powerful, upbeat manner. If you use a breathless whisper or say them halfheartedly, affirmations will not work. It is the power of your intention to believe these statements that makes the affirmations work.

There are many affirmation books available. Check your local library or bookstore. They are usually in the self-help section.

Music

Music is a very powerful mood-altering tool. Music is sound, and it carries an energy vibration. Corporations have spent millions studying various types of music and nature sounds to find out which is the best to sell their products to you on TV or in radio ads, to entice you into their stores, or to keep you captive on their website. National sports teams play upbeat party music during games to make the fans cheer and to encourage the players. You are not a corporation or a sports team, but you can use the same strategy!

Everyone has a favorite genre of music to listen to—rock-n-roll, pop, rap, electronic, metal, country, dance, classical, or new age. Within your favorite genre, you have favorite bands and singers. You spend hundreds of dollars purchasing CDs, concert tickets, and memorabilia on your favorites.

When people are depressed or go through a break up, they tend to listen to love songs or depressing music because it fits the mood they are in. Angry people tend to flock to angry music or lyrics. How do you move from the negative energy of depression, bad mood, or anger?

Make a list of your favorite bands or singers, a list of the ones that really put you in a good mood when you hear their songs. These are your "mood shakers"; they shake you out of a bad mood. These are the songs that you should listen to that will change your attitude and move you out of a funk.

If you are angry all of the time, you may do better changing your music to sound-healing vibrations or music with calming energy. Again, music is vibration and will change the energy around you. That is why holiday music is so popular—it sets a vibrational tone for festivities. Cultural music and national anthems imbues a sense of pride and connection. Children learn better when lessons are applied with music (think of how you learned your ABCs).

Breaking Hexes or Curses

Many people believe in the power of being hexed or cursed. Whether you believe Leslie in accounting hexed you or Jay in your meet-up group cursed you, you are giving power to that thought of being hexed or cursed. If you believe in the possibility of other people hexing or cursing you, you allow their negativity into your life.

There are certain types of people in this world who will actively attempt to hex or curse you due to their jealousy, pettiness, or plain nastiness. These people thrive in darkness and negativity. They will attack you via psychic attacks, energy attacks, or black magic. Just because they send these attacks does not mean they will work. It takes a very skilled person to send a real curse your way.

The best way to handle any type of hex or curse that is sent your way it to NOT allow that person's energy to affect you in any way. Feel free to laugh at someone who says they are going to hex or curse you. That lets them know that you do not believe in their power. You do not have to accept someone else's will or power over you because you have Free Will.

By protecting yourself in the White Light or Robe of Mirrors mentioned in the previous chapter, you are in a protected layer of energy. Stating that you are divinely protected will also keep other people's energy off of you and your business. Stay in the love and light and do not try to send bad energy to that person. Allow Karma to work on them.

If you still feel the need to remove or break a hex or curse, it is best to ask for a referral to someone who is trained in energy cord cutting. They can cut and remove any dark energy from these psychic attacks. You may also call upon your angels to assist in removing dark energies.

Case Studies: Positive Thoughts and Affirmations

Another "a-ha" moment in my classes has always been the part where I explain how your thoughts are energy and you create what you think. Changing the way you think, speak, and act can really make a difference in your life. Here are two student commentaries.

I was really struck with a lightning bolt when you talked about our thoughts and words. I recognized myself during your class as a "Debbie Downer" type with how I spoke to others. It really was affecting me, without my realizing it. I was beginning to wonder why some people were not as available to do things with me. Sometimes they would be really short on the phone with me too.

I have been stuck in this rut of feeling sorry for myself all the time and saying I'm miserable and unlucky to my friends all the time. I can't believe that I'm scaring away my friends. During that moment I listened, I decided I wanted to change so I don't lose my friends. I have really made an effort to think and say things that are more positive. It's hard sometimes, but I do try. I'm feeling better about myself and noticed that I am being invited to my friend's house again. It does feel good!

Kim, Ohio

I always thought it was silly to look in a mirror and say compliments to myself. I know you saw me laugh when you were talking about it. But I figured I would try it and see if it would get me out of my funk. Coming up with nice things to say about myself that first day was hard, but I said I had nice eyes. It was easier the next day when I said I was a good brother, because I know I am.

After that, it was not too hard. If I couldn't think of physical stuff, I'd just say the good brother line. I felt better. So I decided to give compliments to other people that I saw at work or at the gas station. That felt good too.

Scott, Ohio

Part III

WELCOMING POSITIVE ENERGY

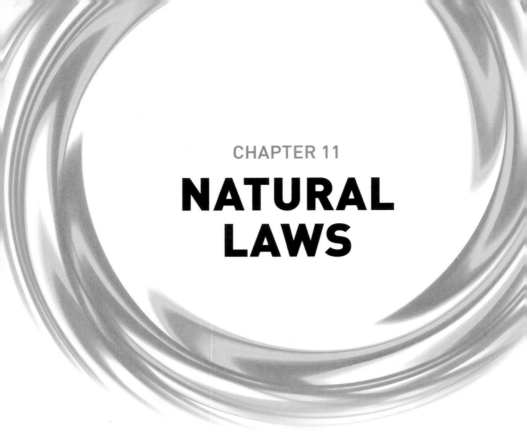

NATURAL LAWS

Natural Laws are the Law of the Universe (or of God—whatever your belief). They operate the same no matter the condition. They are immutable, meaning you cannot change the way they work. Natural laws encompass love, harmony, balance, truth, and vibration. These natural laws now have one superstar among them. This superstar natural law is the Law of Attraction.

Law of Attraction

The most popular and best known of the natural laws is the Law of Attraction. Many people and books teach you how to "attract" things, events, or people to you. They state to just think "positively" and to say positive affirmations, and then you can create everything that you want.

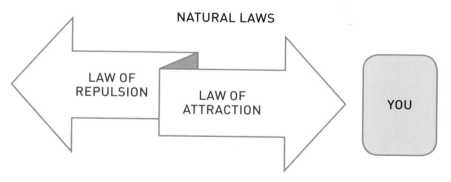

The Law of Attraction BRINGS to you. The Law of Repulsion TAKES from you.

Positive thought patterns will raise your energy vibrations and will assist you in being a magnet for other positive thoughts. They will set your intentions and also make you happier and more open.

That is one part of this law, the most well-known part. However, you also must take action! The second part of this law is not as well known. It is to take action or to create your opportunities. Taking action propels you and your intentions forward. It pulls you out of the static being of just "thinking." Just thinking about something positive will not always bring what you want into your life. The second part of the Law of Attraction is what trips up so many people in manifesting what they want in their lives.

Everyone wants their bliss NOW. Everyone wants to live their dream life NOW. They do not want to actually DO the work or create the action to obtain what they want in their lives. They want others to do the work for them. Taking action or creating opportunities is vitally important to ensure the full Law of Attraction will work with you, your intentions, and your energy.

You currently are an administrative assistant for a doctor. You dream about moving into publishing because you love books. However, you have neither the experience nor the education—whatsoever—in publishing. You may think positively all you want; you may not find a position as a cover designer or editor. You would need to take action! The action required is for you to attend college to obtain your degree. The publishing field requires degrees and experience. You apply to a college and begin night classes.

You also start a job search to make the lateral move as an administrative assistant to a publishing firm. You luck out and become the president's assistant. Now you are working for a publisher and going to college. The Law of Attraction is working for you! Once you take action, this second part of the law will begin working for you to attain your dream position.

Law of Repulsion

For every Natural Law, there is a flip side. Yes, even the Law of Attraction has a flip side! The flip side is the **Law of Repulsion**. When you do not use the Law of Attraction for your highest and greatest good, or you use it to cause harm to someone else, you will then suffer the Law of Repulsion. You could also slip into this law by having desperate, depressed, or angry energy. Your desperation, depression, or anger are negative energies.

What you try to attract instead becomes the thing, event, or person you repel AWAY from you. Why? The Universe (or God) will balance everything out: Those who do not act in a positive manner, do not have a positive intention, or try to do harm instead of good will suffer this karmic effect. It might not be immediate, but it WILL come and then you will see what you worked so hard for slip OUT of your fingers. Think of Karma.

Your negative energy, while attempting to work in the Law of Attraction, will instead create this flip side. If you are desperate, depressed, or angered, your result will be the Law of Repulsion.

EXAMPLE

You are desperate to have a baby. All physical tests show that you can become pregnant with no issues. You time your ovulations, check your husband's sperm count, and schedule sex. Sex becomes a deliberate act to "get pregnant now" instead of the pleasurable connection it should be. You think "baby, baby, baby" during sex instead of how good it feels. Your pregnancy tests always come back negative. Your energy is a frantic, desperate energy, which is now the Law of Repulsion. You are pushing away what you most want—a baby.

Just as easily as it is to slip into the Law of Repulsion—you may also flip that intention back into the Law of Attraction.

EXAMPLE

You realize you are working in the Law of Repulsion. You want to change that energy! So you decide to have an energy healing to align your Chakras. You stop counting and checking ovulations and sperm counts. You decide to have sex for the pleasure of it again. You and your husband have sex in different parts of the house and take a romantic vacation. Sex is now fun and exciting again. You just took action and moved back into the Law of Attraction. Three months later at your OB/GYN appointment, you receive the good news—pregnant!

Just as your thoughts are energy and speaking them amplifies them, your positive actions and intentions will also amplify positive energy. Do not sabotage yourself by not taking action or by living in negative energy. Release desperation, depression, anxiety, and anger from your being. Do you want to attract people, events, and opportunities into your life or do you want to repel them? You have the Free Will to choose.

Flowing in positive energy will assist you in working with all of the natural laws, not just the superstar Law of Attraction.

CHAPTER 12

CREATING POSITIVE ENERGY

The concept of creating positive energy is sometimes astounding to people. Quite frequently, they ask me, "Why do I need to do that?" Once you clear the energy from you, your relationships, your home, yard, and workplace, you will want to raise the energy vibrations. Once negative energy is removed, the energy is now neutral. Neutral energy will attract more neutral energy. Raising the energy vibrations is vitally important. I am going to repeat two very important points.

1. Your thoughts are energy. When you speak those thoughts, they amplify that energy. When you speak to people or about yourself in a positive manner, you amplify positive energy. When you speak to people or about yourself in a negative manner, you amplify negative energy. Your thoughts also set your intentions—whether for the day, week, or year.

2. You live in the energy you are creating. When you strive to be positive in your life, when you act and speak in a positive manner, you are creating positive energy. When you are

CREATING POSITIVE ENERGY

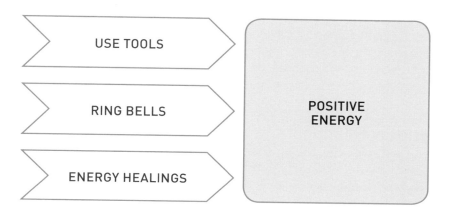

USE TOOLS

RING BELLS

ENERGY HEALINGS

POSITIVE ENERGY

negative, act and speak in a negative manner, you are creating negative energy.

The energy of your being, your thoughts, your words, your intentions, and your actions create the energy that is within you and emanates from you. Your energy will affect everything in your life! As you have read in previous chapters, this energy not only affects you, it also affects your love life, family, friendships, home, yard, and workplace.

You should make every attempt to create positive changes to your thought and behavior patterns. Create powerful, positive intentions to move yourself forward. Train yourself to think, speak, and act in a positive way towards yourself and other people. Remember to say "cancel, clear" whenever you find yourself slipping back into negative patterns.

You may also use the following suggestions to create positive energy.

Previously Discussed Tools

Use some of the tools listed in previous chapters. Light candles or place crystals around your home or other locations. Bathe in sea salts. Sprinkle Melinda's Fairy Dust around your home or workplace to create positive energy. Play upbeat or healing music to fill your space with positive vibrations. Work the Law of Attraction by stating affirmations and taking action.

Ring Bells

You may also go through your home ringing a bell. Bells create sound vibrations—these vibrations are energy. Churches and temples ring bells to call people into their morning services. Governments around the world ring bells for celebrations. You may use any type of bell—crystal, ceramic, brass, or other metals. Ringing a bell in each room will create positive vibrations. These vibrations will fill your space.

Energy Healings

As a spiritual being having a human existence, your body and soul have energy vibrations. Your body has seven main energy points called Chakras. These Chakras are located at your Root, Sacral, Solar Plexus, Heart, Throat, Third Eye, and Crown. Negativity creates energy blockages in your Chakras.

When your Chakras are blocked, your energy is blocked. Make an appointment with an energy healer. The healer may either lay hands over your Chakras or use air symbols, crystals, prayers or meditation to remove the blockages.

There are various types of energy healing. Some of these healings are known as Reiki, Quantum Touch, Integrated Energy Healing, Tapping, or Frequency Therapy. Most healers may be found in holistic centers, metaphysical expos, or stores. Most of the healers you come into contact with will be highly trained and skilled.

I highly suggest that you ask for referrals from family or friends or go to a respected holistic center for energy healings. You do not want an unskilled or poorly trained person working with or manipulating your energy points.

Creating positive energy is simple to do once you have the hang of it. Living in positive energy will calm your emotions and attract more positive energy into your life. You attract what you are; you attract energy at a level that you yourself are vibrating at. What type of vibration do you want to live in? What type of energy do you want emanating from you? What do you want to attract?

We are creating and living in emotions and energies daily. We choose which attitude or mood swing we have on any given day. We want to feel happy, positive, and vibrant. We want to feel alive and joyful. Choose to live and breathe in a positive vibration.

AFTERWORD

You now know the five variants that cause negative energy to enter your life and affect every facet of your being. You are physically and emotionally drained by them. All types of your relationships are impacted by them. The sacred space of your home is destabilized by them. Your career and workplace are weakened by them.

This negativity attracts even more negative energy, people, events, and items into your life. It affects your manifesting abilities. It lowers your energy vibrations. It sabotages you in various ways. It will not leave until you choose to clear it out of your life!

- Will you continue to allow these variants to affect you in such a way?
- Have you recognized yourself in the provided examples within this book?
- Do you wish that your love life is affected by such negativity?
- Will you allow family, friends, and coworkers to participate in negative patterns with you?
- Do you want to remain stuck in a negative energy flow?

If you have answered "NO" to these questions, then you should decide that you WANT to make changes to your thought and behavior patterns starting today.

You now know the free tools you can use to clear the negativity from your life beginning today, right now. You now know the inexpensive tools you can use to clear the negativity from your life. These tools are found in your home, garden, metaphysical shop, or grocery store. Open your refrigerator or cupboard and pull the tools out. Take a trip to your garden center, or your metaphysical or grocery store to pick them up.

You have learned how to use each of these tools to clear the negative energy out of your life. You also know HOW you may create positive energy, starting right now. Positive energy will attract more positive energy, people, events, opportunities, and items into your life.

It all begins with YOU! You create your own energy. The energy emanating from you is what other people in your life react to. You participate in creating energy with others, whether a lover, a family member, a friend, or a coworker.

Choose to live in a positive energy flow. Choose to create positive thoughts, intentions, and behavior patterns in your life today. It is your opportunity, right now, to allow these changes in your life.

Life is beautiful. The opportunity to live right now in positive energy is yours. Your life may become more beautiful to you. Your life may be more joyous and fulfilling. It begins with you right now. Make your life beautiful, allow joy to vibrate, and feel fulfilled. Choose to live in a positive energy flow today.

Get positive, live positive!

GET POSITIVE, LIVE POSITIVE WORKSHEET

Your thoughts are energy. Every time you speak them, you amplify that energy. To assist you in creating a new pattern of thought, use this worksheet, based on Chapter 10. This exercise will help you to see in black and white your feelings, thoughts, and desires. It will showcase the steps you have decided to use to improve your life. I want you to Get Positive, Live Positive! Space has been provided for you to write your answers.

1. These are my positive thoughts about my physical self:

_____

_____

_____

_____

_____

_____

2. These are my positive thoughts about my personality:

_____

_____

_____

_____

_____

_____

3. People give me compliments all the time about:

_____

_____

_____

_____

_____

4. I notice and compliment others about:

_____

_____

_____

_____

_____

5. My most positive relationship in life is with:

_____

_____

_____

_____

_____

6. The reason(s) why this is my most positive relationship is (are):

_____

_____

_____

_____

_____

_____

7. I cherish this person and work to keep this relationship positive because:

_____

_____

_____

_____

_____

_____

8. My most negative relationship in life is with:

_____

_____

_____

_____

_____

_____

9. The reason(s) why this is my most negative relationship:

_____

_____

_____

_____

_____

_____

10. I like this person and want to improve this relationship because:

_____

_____

_____

_____

_____

_____

11. I dislike this person and will sever this relationship because:

_____

_____

_____

_____

_____

_____

12. These are the items that I want to change about my personal life:

_____

_____

_____

_____

_____

_____

13. This is the step(s) I need to take to make that change:

_____

_____

_____

_____

_____

_____

14. I am creating this positive boundary to handle my personal life:

_____

_____

_____

_____

_____

_____

15. These are the items that I would like to see change about my career:

_____

_____

_____

_____

_____

16. This is the step(s) I need to take to make that change:

_____

_____

_____

_____

_____

17. I am creating this positive boundary to handle my work life:

_____

_____

_____

_____

_____

18. This is the energy vibration that I want in my home:

_____

_____

_____

_____

_____

19. This is the step(s) I need to take to make that change:

_____

_____

_____

_____

_____

20. I am creating this positive boundary for my home:

_____

_____

_____

_____

_____

21. I will stop saying this negative comment about myself:

_____

_____

_____

_____

_____

22. I will replace that comment with this positive thought:

_____

_____

_____

_____

_____

23. I will stop saying this negative comment about my partner:

_____

_____

_____

_____

_____

24. I will replace that comment with this positive thought:

_____

_____

_____

_____

_____

_____

25. I will stop saying this negative comment about my family:

_____

_____

_____

_____

_____

_____

26. I will replace that comment with this positive thought:

_____

_____

_____

_____

_____

_____

27. I will stop saying this negative comment about my career:

_____

_____

_____

_____

_____

28. I will replace that comment with this positive thought:

_____

_____

_____

_____

_____

29. I am grateful for the following people in my life:

_____

_____

_____

_____

_____

_____

30. I am grateful for the following items in my life:

_____

_____

_____

_____

_____

_____

31. I rejoice that I have:

_____

_____

_____

_____

_____

32. My thoughts are energy; I amplify that energy when I speak.

_____

_____

_____

_____

_____

_____

33. I am going to get positive and to live positive, starting today.

_____

_____

_____

_____

_____

_____

14 TIPS TO BECOME A MORE POSITIVE PERSON

Many people have attended my workshops through the years and regularly ask me for tips and advice to improve their energy or help them to be more positive. Here is an article I wrote for my monthly newsletter a couple of years ago.

Would you like to become a more positive person?

How do you begin? You do not have to be stuck in negative energy. Changing your thought and behavior patterns will assist you in turning your energy around. By becoming a positive person, you will attract positive energy, events, opportunities,and people into your life. Try one or more of these tips.

Begin by smiling.

Smiling at other people makes you more approachable and likeable. It also makes others smile back at you. Smiling is a friendly exchange of energy.

Say "Thank You" and mean it!

Anytime someone performs a service for you, thank them. This acknowledgment is important; so many people do not thank the people in their life who help them.

Mail a letter or card to the troops.

Letters and cards from home are the biggest morale boost to the men and women serving far from home. Visit the United Service Organization (USO) website for information: www.uso.org

Take a walk in the woods with a friend.

Getting out into nature helps to rebalance your energy. Nature is beautiful—the flowers, trees, and the antics of small animals can make you laugh. Breathe in all around you and feel your spirit calm down.

Prayer or meditation.

Prayer is your opportunity to speak to God, Goddess, or the Universe. Meditation is your opportunity to listen to God, Goddess, or the Universe. By doing both of these regularly, you will connect to the Divine and allow the Divine within you to feel blessed.

Go to a carnival.

Let your inner child out! Have fun with your partner, family, or friends by going on a ride, eating cotton candy, or playing games. By playing and laughing, you will bring joy back into your life.

Splurge on yourself.

Sometimes you are so busy taking care of children, parents, or friends you forget to take care of yourself. Running yourself ragged depletes your energy. Take as little as ten minutes out of your day to have an ice cream cone, or go for a manicure, or buy yourself something nice. Splurging on yourself every now and then boosts your energy back up.

Go to the beach.

Spend a day at the beach swimming and feeling the sand in between your toes. Allow the sun to shine on you. This is a great way to release stress. Watching and listening to the sound of the waves are good ways to calm yourself and to connect with nature.

Change your body's energy.

Energy healings are a wonderful treatment to adjust your body's energy and to align your Chakras. They remove blockages in your Chakras and assist in emotional and physical healing. Try Energy Cord Cutting, Reiki, Quantum Touch, or Tapping treatments.

Donate items.

When you help the less fortunate, it makes you feel good. Women's and homeless shelters always welcome clothing, toys, and body and hair products. Purple Heart will take gently used clothing and small appliances. Harvest for Hunger accepts canned and boxed food. These shelters and organizations (and others in your local area) are listed in your local phone book or online.

Meet new people—volunteer!

By joining a group that is involved in a good cause, you will bring new people and experiences into your life. This assists you in changing any stagnant energy in your life. You may also join a local metaphysical club or meet-up group.

Help someone in need.

While you are at a store or an event, if you see someone struggling—help them! If it's an older person having a hard time lifting items from their cart, offer to lift the items for them. If someone asks you for assistance, don't ignore them, help them! By helping someone in need, you are giving back to the universe.

Affirmations.

Stating positive affirmations will boost your energy and assist you in changing your thought patterns. Your thoughts are energy, and stating them amplifies that energy. Affirmations are a simple, effective way to help you bring positive change into your life.

Adopt a pet.

Pet shelters and animal rescues across the nation are overflowing with unwanted dogs, cats, and other pets. A pet will bring you unconditional love and companionship. Petting a dog or cat has been scientifically proven to lower blood pressure. By adopting an animal in need, you give the gift of life and a secure home for these animals. Call or visit your local shelters or rescue groups to find the right pet for you.

By changing small things in your thought or behavior patterns in a positive manner, you affect your life greatly. Allow positive energy into your life.

SHOPPING LIST OF TOOLS

The following list of tools will assist you while shopping at your grocery store, garden center, or metaphysical store.

Tools in Your Grocery Store

✓	Product	Notes
	Fresh Lemon	
	Bottled Lemon Juice	
	Sea Salt	
	Other	

Tools at Your Garden Center

✓	Product	Notes
	Sage	
	Lavender	
	Lemon Balm	
	Other	

Tools at Your Metaphysical Store

✓	Product	Notes
	Copal Resin Incense	
	Charcoal	
	Sage Bundle or Smudge	
	Melinda's Cosmic Dust	
	Candle (White)	
	Candle (Yellow)	
	Candle (Green)	
	Melinda's Fairy Dust	
	Clear Quartz Crystal	
	Rose Quartz Crystal	
	Amethyst (8 pieces)	
	Selenite	
	Other	

AFFIRMATION CARDS

I have listed below five of my affirmations from Chapter 10 for your use. If you would like to carry them with you, photocopy or cut them out, or retype them as large as you like. Attaching them or typing them onto index cards will make them more sturdy.

A. I act in a positive manner with positive energy flowing into my life in all directions.

B. My energy is aligned with the Divine and I flow in love, light, abundance, and positive energy.

C. My life is full of positive energy, laughter, gifts, blessings, and joy.

D. I am open and worthy of all that the Universe has to offer, and I accept these wonderful gifts now.

E. My possibilities are endless: I create them, I see them!

RECIPES TO CREATE POSITIVE ENERGY

Here are two of my recipes that you may use to attract positive energy and abundance into your life. The ingredients are already in your spice cupboard or local metaphysical store.

Prosperity

You may use this recipe to welcome prosperity into your life.

Ingredients:
¼ teaspoon brown sugar
¼ teaspoon cinnamon

Directions:
Mix equal parts of a quarter teaspoon each of brown sugar and cinnamon in a small bowl. Open your front door. Using your left hand, sprinkle the mixture outside saying,

"Prosperity is welcome to come in."

You may also sprinkle some in your wallet to bring prosperity. It is best to complete this action on a Thursday, which is ruled by the Roman god Jupiter. Jupiter is known for bringing good fortune and increasing opportunities.

Super-Charged Positive Energy Mix

This super-charged mix combines the negative energy clearing abilities of sea salt, sage, and Cosmic Dust with the positive energy vibration of the Fairy Dust. It is wonderful to use as a ward for your property and to attract opportunities to you. This mixture may also be used at any business location.

Ingredients:
Sea salt
Sage leaves (crushed)
Melinda's Fairy Dust
Melinda's Cosmic Dust

Directions:
Mix equal parts sea salt, crushed sage leaves, Melinda's Fairy Dust, and Melinda's Cosmic Dust in a bowl. Scatter the mixture around your property line and the four outside corners of your home or other location.

Positive Energy for Job Searches

Looking for a new job or changing careers is often a long process. Many people send dozens of resumes to companies. Some people are interviewed three times before a company will make a job offer. Rejections from these companies can impact you emotionally. In today's tight job market, every bit of positive energy will assist you in your search. Here is a tip that I have provided quite often on my radio show to those looking for a job to create positive energy.

In the days before computers and e-mails, people would type their resume on a typewriter, then fold it and stuff it in an envelope. They would then mail the resume to a company. The resume was infused by the job seeker's energy. In today's world, we e-mail resumes or are stuck copying and pasting parts of resumes into the company's website. Resumes are no longer infused with energy. Here are some ways to infuse your energy into your resume:

Requires:
Printed copy of resume
Pen/pencil
Tea light or chime candle in white or green (may also use a taper or votive)
Candle holder

Directions:
1. Print a copy of your resume.
2. Write on the back, "I have a wonderful job." You do not want

to write "looking for," or "searching for." Those are negative energy vibrations and will keep you looking and searching.

3. Under the above statement, you will write what you are hopeful for: good pay and benefits, wonderful coworkers, professional atmosphere, etc.

4. Next, light a white candle (for new beginnings and the Universal light) or light a green candle (for abundance and prosperity). It is best to use a tea light candle or chime candle. They are quick burning. However, you may also use a taper or votive candle.

5. State out loud the comments you have written on the back of your resume.

6. Place the candle on top of your resume (in a safe candle holder) and allow it to burn completely.

You may do this once a week or more often depending on the energy you need to create.

Archangel Michael

I have enjoyed seeing and speaking to Archangel Michael since I was a child. He is my very favorite Archangel. Archangels are the largest, strongest, and most powerful of the angels. He is the right hand of God and Goddess. He is the Protector of the Realm and vanquishes darkness, evil, and negativity. With Archangel Michael, not only is he the strongest of all the angels, he is the one with the best sense of humor.

He is the one I work the most closely with and has appeared to me many times at turning points in my life (like my story in the Preface). He has also appeared at times when I've needed a power boost when helping others, provided healing energy to me, or if I needed extra protection.

Most people see angels as all fluffy feathers and halos, singing on clouds. I personally never saw Archangel Michael on a cloud. He just appears larger than life in front of me in my home or other location. I know I can count on him to appear whenever I call upon him. His energy is the darkest sapphire blue. The warmth and love that emanates from him is one vibration below the Divine God and Goddess. He represents Divine Energy, love, security, and yes, even joy to me.

Please do not hesitate to call upon him in your times of need. You will feel his divine blue warmth as he removes fear, doubt, negativity, or darkness. Archangel Michael answers every call made upon him. Just ask and he will appear.

Archangel Michael has given me many messages for myself and for others in my sessions with clients through the past years. He occasionally provides a worldwide message to me. I would like to share one of my favorites with you below. His message never fails to boost my energy and remind me of my Divine Spark.

Channeled Message from Archangel Michael

I originally received this worldwide message from Archangel Michael in February 2014 and published it in my March 2014 newsletter, *Positive Perspectives*. It will speak to your soul.

Love and greetings dear Children of God and Goddess. I am the Right Hand of God and Goddess that protects their Kingdom from the darkness. Call upon me when you are lost; I will lead the way into the Light. Call upon me to protect you from fear; my wings will bring you warmth and give you strength. Call upon me to defend you from the dark energy that tries to diminish your Divine Spark. I will smite the darkness with my sword, and it will no longer surround you. No plea is too small to ask.

You dear one, are a beloved Child of God and Goddess. You have only to ask and I will be right beside you, bringing their love and light to flow around and within you. My blue light ray surrounds and protects you, guiding you and your prayers to the ears of God and Goddess. I am Archangel Michael, sworn protector of their kingdom. They are the Love, the Power, and the Glory. Feel their great love within you—accept their Divine Blessings. May you know that I am here to love, heal, and protect you.

RESOURCES

The following is a listing of locations that offer my products.

Colorado
For Heaven's Sake Books—Denver
Full Moon Books & Event Center—Denver
Shining Lotus Metaphysical Books—Denver

Kansas
White Dove—Wichita

Ohio
Crystal Era—Elyria
Divine Awakenings—Sandusky
Goddess Blessed—Lakewood
It's Your Journey—Huron
Mystic Imports—Cleveland

South Dakota
Sturgis T-Shirts & Gifts—Sturgis

Online
Melinda's Website—www.psychicmelinda.webs.com
Pagan Presence—www.paganpresence.com
Amazon—www.amazon.com

To read testimonials relating to the effectiveness of Melinda Carver products, visit www.psychicmelinda.webs.com.

INDEX

Note Pages

Note Pages